GREAT BOOKS OF THE WESTERN WORLD

Introductory Volumes:

1. The Great Conversation

2. The Great Ideas I

3. The Great Ideas II

4. HOMER

5. AESCHYLUS
   SOPHOCLES
   EURIPIDES
   ARISTOPHANES

6. HERODOTUS
   THUCYDIDES

7. PLATO

8. ARISTOTLE I

9. ARISTOTLE II

10. HIPPOCRATES
    GALEN

11. EUCLID
    ARCHIMEDES
    APOLLONIUS
    NICOMACHUS

12. LUCRETIUS
    EPICTETUS
    MARCUS AURELIUS

13. VIRGIL

14. PLUTARCH

15. TACITUS

16. PTOLEMY
    COPERNICUS
    KEPLER

17. PLOTINUS

18. AUGUSTINE

19. THOMAS AQUINAS I

20. THOMAS AQUINAS II

21. DANTE

22. CHAUCER

23. MACHIAVELLI
    HOBBES

24. RABELAIS

25. MONTAIGNE

26. SHAKESPEARE I

27. SHAKESPEARE II

GREAT BOOKS OF THE WESTERN WORLD

28. GILBERT
    GALILEO
    HARVEY

29. CERVANTES

30. FRANCIS BACON

31. DESCARTES
    SPINOZA

32. MILTON

33. PASCAL

34. NEWTON
    HUYGENS

35. LOCKE
    BERKELEY
    HUME

36. SWIFT
    STERNE

37. FIELDING

38. MONTESQUIEU
    ROUSSEAU

39. ADAM SMITH

40. GIBBON I

41. GIBBON II

42. KANT

43. AMERICAN STATE
    PAPERS
    THE FEDERALIST
    J. S. MILL

44. BOSWELL

45. LAVOISIER
    FOURIER
    FARADAY

46. HEGEL

47. GOETHE

48. MELVILLE

49. DARWIN

50. MARX
    ENGELS

51. TOLSTOY

52. DOSTOEVSKY

53. WILLIAM JAMES

54. FREUD

Archbishop Mitty High School
Media Center
5000 Mitty Way
San Jose, CA   95129

RULES

1. All pupils in the school are entitled to use the library and to borrow books.
2. Reserved books may be borrowed for one period, or at the close of school, and should be returned before the first class the following school day.
3. All other books may be retained for two weeks.
4. Injury to books beyond reasonable wear and all losses shall be paid for.
5. No books may be taken from the library without being charged.

GREAT BOOKS
OF THE WESTERN WORLD

ROBERT MAYNARD HUTCHINS, *EDITOR IN CHIEF*

I.

THE GREAT CONVERSATION

MORTIMER J. ADLER, *Associate Editor*

Members of the Advisory Board: STRINGFELLOW BARR, SCOTT BUCHANAN, JOHN ERSKINE, CLARENCE H. FAUST, ALEXANDER MEIKLEJOHN, JOSEPH J. SCHWAB, MARK VAN DOREN.

Editorial Consultants: A. F. B. CLARK, F. L. LUCAS, WALTER MURDOCH.

WALLACE BROCKWAY, *Executive Editor*

THE
GREAT CONVERSATION
The Substance of a Liberal Education

BY ROBERT M. HUTCHINS

WILLIAM BENTON, *Publisher*

ENCYCLOPÆDIA BRITANNICA, INC.

CHICAGO · LONDON · TORONTO · GENEVA · SYDNEY · TOKYO · MANILA

The quotations, with permission, used by Mr. Hutchins in this volume are from the following sources:

Aims of Education by Alfred N. Whitehead (The Macmillan Company, 1929)

Am I My Brother's Keeper? by Ananda K. Coomaraswamy (The John Day Company Inc., 1947)

Democracy and Education by John Dewey (The Macmillan Company, 1916)

On Education by Sir Richard Livingstone (Cambridge University Press, 1944)

On Understanding Science by James B. Conant (Yale University Press, 1947)

Selected Essays by T. S. Eliot (Harcourt, Brace and Company, Inc., 1950)

"Social Science Among the Humanities" by Robert Redfield, in *Measure*, vol. 1, no. 1 (Henry Regnery Company, 1950)

Quotations from Louis W. Norris and John D. Wild are from comments in *Goals For American Education* (The Conference on Science, Philosophy and Religion in Their Relation to the Democratic Way of Life, Inc., distributed by Harper & Brothers, 1950)

THE UNIVERSITY OF CHICAGO

The Great Books
is published with the editorial advice of the faculties
of The University of Chicago

©

1952
BY ENCYCLOPÆDIA BRITANNICA, INC.
TWENTY-SEVENTH PRINTING, 1984

COPYRIGHT UNDER INTERNATIONAL COPYRIGHT UNION

ALL RIGHTS RESERVED UNDER PAN AMERICAN AND UNIVERSAL COPYRIGHT CONVENTIONS BY ENCYCLOPÆDIA BRITANNICA, INC.

Library of Congress Catalog Card Number: 55-10312
International Standard Book Number: 0-85229-163-9

☆ Great Books of the Western World

ROBERT MAYNARD HUTCHINS, *Editor*

MORTIMER J. ADLER, *Associate Editor*

Members of the Advisory Board

STRINGFELLOW BARR, Professor of History in the University of Virginia, and formerly President of St. John's College in Annapolis, Maryland

SCOTT BUCHANAN, philosopher, and formerly Dean of St. John's College

JOHN ERSKINE, novelist, and formerly Professor of English in Columbia University

CLARENCE FAUST, President of the Fund for the Advancement of Education, and formerly Dean of the Humanities and Sciences in Leland Stanford University

ALEXANDER MEIKLEJOHN, philosopher, and formerly Chairman of the School for Social Studies in San Francisco

JOSEPH SCHWAB, scientist, and Professor in the College of the University of Chicago

MARK VAN DOREN, poet, and Professor of English in Columbia University

Editorial Consultants

CANADA: A. F. B. CLARK, Professor of French Literature in the University of British Columbia, Canada

ENGLAND: F. L. LUCAS, Fellow and Lecturer of King's College, Cambridge, England

AUSTRALIA: WALTER MURDOCH, Professor of English Literature in the University of Western Australia

℣ Great Books of the Western World

THIS PRIVATE LIBRARY EDITION
of Great Books of the Western World *was originally
made possible in 1952 by the generous support of the subscribers
to the Founders' Edition. The Publisher and Editors are grate-
ful to those who, by their subscription at a cost of $500 a set
to the limited Founders' Edition of 500 sets, facilitated the
general publication of these books.*

*In addition to individual persons, the subscription list in-
cluded business corporations and educational institutions—libraries or schools. Some subscribers purchased sets for themselves
and some donated the sets they purchased to educational institutions.*

*Listed below are the names of the subscribers to, and the donors
and recipients of, the Founders' Edition of* Great Books *of the*
Western World. *The names of a certain number of subscribers
and donors have been withheld at their request. The listing is
divided into the following four groups:*

I. Individual Persons who subscribed to one or
    more sets for themselves or for donation to
    educational institutions

II. Business Corporations which subscribed to sets
    for their own use or for donation to educa-
    tional institutions

III. Educational Institutions which subscribed to sets for their own use, and philanthropic organizations which donated sets to educational institutions

IV. Educational Institutions which have been designated as recipients of gift sets

In the first three lists an asterisk after the name of the person, business corporation, or philanthropic organization indicates subscribers to two or more sets, or donors of sets to educational institutions. Except for those whose names are withheld at their request, the names of donors are indicated in the fourth list in parentheses after the name of the educational institution which received the gift set from them.

❊ I ❊

John Charles Acton

Mrs. Sarah Wood Addington

James F. Albright

Bernice Wells Aldridge

Dr. Hector M. Davila Alonso

Charles Lesley Ames

Clinton P. Anderson*

J. M. Arvey

C. H. Babcock

George Backer

George F. Baker, Jr.*

Mrs. James H. Becker

Paul E. Becker

S. N. Behrman

Laird Bell

The Rt. Hon. David Ben-Gurion

Mr. and Mrs. Clayton W. Bernhardt*

Philip Case Biggert

Walter R. Bimson

Mrs. Tiffany Blake*

Mr. and Mrs. Carleton Blunt*

CORWIN HEFRIGHT BOATE

GEORGE C. BOLIAN II

J. A. BOLZ, M.D.

EDWIN G. BOOZ

FREDERIC M. BOSWORTH*

SCOTT BUCHANAN*

WALTHER BUCHEN

BRITTON I. BUDD*

LEO BURNETT

Mrs. ADELAIDE CAMERON

FRANK CAPRA

Mrs. JOHN ALDEN CARPENTER

ALFRED T. CARTON*

Rev. CHARLES S. CASASSA, S.J.

JOSEPH and MARGARET CHADWICK

Mrs. GILBERT W. CHAPMAN

ALFREDO CHAVERO

JOHN TIMOTHY CHORD

JACK F. CHRYSLER

CARLETON A. CLEVELAND*

EDWARD L. CLISSOLD

Mr. and Mrs. MARVIN H. COLEMAN

EDWARD LYON COMPERE, M.D.

FAIRFAX M. CONE

JOHN COWLES*

ABRAHAM M. DAVIS

J. LIONBERGER DAVIS*

E. DEGOLYER*

EDISON DICK*

Mr. and Mrs. GAYLORD DONNELLEY

Mr. and Mrs. JAMES H. DOUGLAS, Jr.

GORDON DUKE

ALFRED K. EDDY*

C. FRASER ELLIOTT, C.M.G., K.C.

Mrs. ARTHUR E. ENGLISH*

MAX EPSTEIN

ARMAND GROVER ERPF

D. C. EVEREST*

Dr. HAROLD E. FARMER

MILLARD C. FAUGHT

HARRY G. FERNQUIST

MARSHALL FIELD

MARSHALL FIELD, Jr.

RICHARD J. FINNEGAN

CLARK W. FINNERUD, M.D

MORRIS FISHBEIN, M.D.

LOUIS WILLIAM FORREY

CHARLES Y. FREEMAN*

Mr. and Mrs. A. J. Freiler

Edward P. Gallagher

Edward F. Gallahue

Mr. and Mrs. Robert W. Galvin

Mr. and Mrs. Otto Emil Geppert

Mr. and Mrs. Gerald S. Gidwitz

A. M. Gilbert

Alfred C. Glassell, Jr.

Richard E. Gold

Joel Goldblatt

William T. Golden

Benedict K. Goodman

Pierre F. Goodrich*

Albert H. Gordon

Edward R. Gould

Charles M. Grace*

Mr. and Mrs. Alan R. Graff

Henry S. Griffing

Vicente Leon Guerrero

Eunice F. Hale*

Jake L. Hamon

Irving Brooks Harris

Dr. Emil D. W. Hauser

R. E. Havenstrite

WILL H. HAYS

Dr. and Mrs. PAUL G. HENLEY

BURNS HENRY, Jr.

HENRY H. HILL

CONRAD N. HILTON

WM. A. HIRSH, Jr.

OVETA CULP HOBBY

PAUL G. HOFFMAN

ALBERT L. HOPKINS

Mr. and Mrs. CYRIL O. HOULE

G. T. HOWSON and J. H. MICHENER*

A. NORMAN INTO*

Sr. MANUEL SENDEROS IRIGOYEN

R. G. IVEY

PROEHL HALLER JAKLON

SIDNEY L. JAMES

Mr. and Mrs. MERLIN E. JOHNSON

Col. KILBOURNE JOHNSTON, U.S.A. (Ret.)

Mr. and Mrs. J. LEDDY JONES*

Mr. and Mrs. JACK S. JOSEY

Mr. and Mrs. WILLIAM H. JOYCE, Jr.

GEORGE T. KEATING*

JOHN E. KENNEY

MEYER KESTNBAUM

WILLARD V. KING*

GEOFFREY KNIGHT

JOHN S. KNIGHT

R. C. KRAMER*

ROY E. LARSEN

SAM LAUD

MARC A. LAW

DR. THEODORE K. LAWLESS

JEFFREY L. LAZARUS

FOREMAN M. LEBOLD*

DAVID LESTER

HENRY R. LEVY*

ISAAC D. LEVY*

CHARLES W. LEWIS

HAROLD F. LINDER*

WALTER LIPPMANN

GLEN A. LLOYD*

MR. AND MRS. HENRY A. LOEB*

JOHN LANGELOTH LOEB*

NANNA RASMUSSEN LOTHE

IRWIN J. LUBBERS

HENRY R. LUCE

HUGHSTON M. McBAIN

CHARLES E. McCARTHY

FOWLER McCORMICK

JOHN WRIGHT McGHEE

ARTHUR B. McGLOTHLAN, M.D., F.A.C.R.

EARLE McKAY

ZACHARY McKAY

Mr. and Mrs. GEORGE B. McKIBBIN*

ALAN ROBERT McNABB

ANDREW McNALLY III

LEWIS W. MacNAUGHTON

JOHN W. MALONEY*

FRED L. MANDEL, Jr.

Col. LEON MANDEL

JOSEPH L. MANKIEWICZ

JAMES A. MARKLE

WIRT P. MARKS, Jr.

ARTHUR F. MARQUETTE

Mr. and Mrs. SAMUEL A. MARX

MORTON D. MAY

PAUL MELLON*

Mrs. THOMAS A. MELLON*

JOHN P. MENTZER

Dr. HENRY MEZGER

OLIUS P. MICHAELS

MARVIN MILLSAP

Mr. and Mrs. Carleton Mitchell

Mrs. Charlotte I. Morse

Bernard Mortimer

Sol Morton

Carl E. Moses

Robert C. Munnecke

Elbert Haven Neese

Walter Gustav Nelson

John Nuveen

Mr. and Mrs. J. Sanford Otis

Walter P. Paepcke

William S. Paley

Mrs. Potter Palmer

Thomas Parran, M.D.*

Miss Alicia Patterson

Robert Pollak*

Ronald Price, M.D.

George E. Probst

Andrew E. Propper

B. Earl Puckett

Ernest E. Quantrell

Henry Regnery

Ethel Linder Reiner

Raymond H. Reiss

HERMAN HENRY RIDDER

GEORGE RIEVESCHL, JR.

JOEL ROCHA, JR.

Mrs. WILLIAM M. ROGERS

CHARLES J. ROSENBLOOM*

M. A. ROSENTHAL

LESSING J. ROSENWALD

GEORGE W. ROSSETTER

RAYMOND RUBICAM

ARTHUR L. H. RUBIN*

Mrs. CLIVE RUNNELLS*

ROBERT J. RUSH

Mrs. PAUL S. RUSSELL

WM. J. SAMFORD

HARRY W. SCHACTER

HARRY SCHERMAN*

SYDNEY K. SCHIFF

WILLEM C. SCHILTHUIS

ADOLPH W. SCHMIDT

M. LINCOLN SCHUSTER

CHARLES WARD SEABURY

Mr. and Mrs. GEORGE L. SEATON

LESTER N. SELIG

JOHN LAWSON SENIOR, JR.

ALFRED SHAW

WILFRED L. SHEA

Mr. and Mrs. RENSLOW P. SHERER*

LEO J. SHERIDAN

WICKLIFFE SHREVE

HENRY CARLTON SHULL*

Mr. and Mrs. LOUIS H. SILVER*

JOHN L. SIMPSON

TOM SLICK

RALPH H. SMALE

WILLIAM A. SMITH

TRUE E. SNOWDEN*

Mr. and Mrs. JOHN V SPACHNER

A. N. SPANEL*

ALBERT B. SPECTOR

LEO SPITZ*

THOS. G. STALEY

Mr. and Mrs. W. T. STALTER*

Mr. and Mrs. JAY Z. STEINBERG

Mr. and Mrs. WILLIAM SHERMAN STREET

Mrs. RALPH SULLIVANT

ELBERT GARY SUTCLIFFE*

Mrs. ALDEN B. SWIFT

CLAIRE D. SWIFT*

HAROLD H. SWIFT*

H. J. SZOLD*

MAURICE JOSEPH TAYLOR, M.D.

M. E. TRAPP, Jr.

DONALD S. TRUMBULL*

ADOLPH ULLMAN

ALFRED G. VANDERBILT

GALEN VAN METER

ROBERT and ANNE VAN VALKENBURGH

CHARLES VIDOR

Dr. HAROLD C. VORIS

CHARLES R. WALGREEN, Jr.

WILLIAM M. WARD

GEORGE H. WATKINS

JAMES B. WEBBER, Jr.

RICHARD WEIL, Jr.

ERIC W. WEINMANN

DONALD P. WELLES

EDWARD K. WELLES

ROBERT AVERY WHITNEY

LOUIS STODDARD WILDER

Mrs. LYNN A. WILLIAMS

RAYMOND H. WITTCOFF

MAX WOOLPY

THOMAS R. YGLESIAS
JAMES WEBB YOUNG*
BEN D. ZEVIN
HERBERT P. ZIMMERMANN
ESTHER SOMERFELD-ZISKIND, M.D., and
 EUGENE ZISKIND, M.D.

❦ II ❧

American Typesetting Corporation, *Chicago, Illinois*
C. C. Anderson Company, *Boise, Idaho**
C. C. Anderson Company, *Ogden, Utah**
Arthur Young & Company, *Chicago, Illinois*
Barnes-Woodin, *Yakima, Washington**
The Bon Marché, *Everett, Washington**
The Bon Marché, *Longview, Washington**
The Bon Marché, *Spokane, Washington**
The Bon Marché, *Tacoma, Washington**
The Bon Marché, *Walla Walla, Washington**
The Bon Ton, *Lebanon, Pennsylvania**
Container Corporation of America, *Chicago, Illinois*
Converse Rubber Corporation, *Malden, Massachusetts*
Courier Journal & Louisville Times, *Louisville, Kentucky*
Dey Bros. & Company, *Syracuse, New York**
L. S. Donaldson Company, *Rapid City, South Dakota**
Doubleday & Company, Inc., *New York, New York*
The L. H. Field Company, *Jackson, Michigan**
Geneva Steel Company, *Geneva, Utah**
Hardy-Herpolsheimer Company, *Muskegon, Michigan**
Heer's, Inc., *Springfield, Missouri**

Herpolsheimer Company, *Grand Rapids, Michigan**

Joske's of Texas, *San Antonio, Texas**

Kennecott Copper Corporation, Chino Mines Division, *Hurley, New Mexico**

Wm. Laubach & Sons, *Easton, Pennsylvania**

Maas Bros., *Tampa, Florida**

Marshall Field & Company, *Chicago, Illinois*

Metzger-Wright Company, *Warren, Pennsylvania**

The Meyer's Company, *Greensboro, North Carolina**

Michigan National Bank, *Lansing, Michigan**

The Muller Company, Ltd., *Lake Charles, Louisiana**

The Paris of Montana, *Great Falls, Montana**

The Parker Pen Company, *Janesville, Wisconsin*

Pepperidge Farm, Inc., *Norwalk, Connecticut*

The Philadelphia Inquirer, Walter H. Annenberg, Editor and Publisher, *Philadelphia, Pennsylvania*

A. Polsky & Company, *Akron, Ohio**

Pomeroy's, Inc., *Pottsville, Pennsylvania**

Pomeroy's, Inc., *Wilkes-Barre, Pennsylvania**

Potash Company of America, *Carlsbad, New Mexico**

Quackenbush Company, *Paterson, New Jersey**

The Rollman & Sons Company, *Cincinnati, Ohio**

Salomon Bros. & Hutzler, *New York, New York**

Standard Oil Company (Indiana), *Chicago, Illinois*

Sterling-Lindner-Davis Company, *Cleveland Ohio**
Time Inc., Library, *New York, New York*
The Titche-Goettinger Company, *Dallas, Texas**
A. E. Troutman Company, *Greensburg, Pennsylvania**
A. E. Troutman Company, *Indiana, Pennsylvania**
United States Potash Company, *New York, New York**
Westinghouse Educational Center, *Wilkinsburg,*
    Pennsylvania

❖ III ❖

Bates College, *Lewiston, Maine*

Champlain College Library, State University of New York, *Plattsburg, New York*

Colleges of the Seneca: Hobart College, William Smith College, *Geneva, New York*

The Cranbrook Foundation, *Bloomfield Hills, Michigan*

Department of Education (Mariano Villaronga, Commissioner of Education), *San Juan, Puerto Rico*

Department of Social Sciences, United States Military Academy, *West Point, New York*

Detroit Public Library, *Detroit, Michigan*

Erin Bain Jones Library of Comparative Literature, Southern Methodist University, *Dallas, Texas*

The Fund for Adult Education, *Pasadena, California*

The Fund for the Advancement of Education, *New York, New York*

Friends of Charles H. Compton, *St. Louis, Missouri**

Friends of the Oak Park Library, *Oak Park, Illinois**

Gertrude Kistler Memorial Library, Rosemont College, *Rosemont, Pennsylvania*

Great Books Discussion Leaders, *Berkeley, California**

Huntington Hartford Foundation, *Pacific Palisades, California*

Illinois State Library, *Springfield, Illinois*

Iwate University, *Morioka, Japan*

Kent State University Library, *Kent, Ohio*

The Library, Southwestern at Memphis, *Memphis, Tennessee*

Lincoln Library, *Springfield, Illinois*

Marquette University, *Milwaukee, Wisconsin*

Minneapolis Athenaeum, *Minneapolis, Minnesota*

Northern Illinois State Teachers College, *De Kalb, Illinois*

North Texas State College Library, *Denton, Texas*

Oklahoma City Libraries, *Oklahoma City, Oklahoma*

Purdue University Libraries, *Lafayette, Indiana*

The Robert D. Sanders Foundation, *Jackson, Mississippi**

St. Mary's College of California, *Saint Mary's College, California*

.St. Paul Public Library, *St. Paul, Minnesota*

St. Vincent College Library, *Latrobe, Pennsylvania*

Southern Illinois University Libraries, *Carbondale, Illinois*

Stephens Memorial Library, Southwestern Louisiana Institute, *Lafayette, Louisiana*

Texas Technological College, *Lubbock, Texas*

University of Notre Dame, *Notre Dame, Indiana*
University of Utah Library, *Salt Lake City, Utah*
Valparaiso University, *Valparaiso, Indiana*
Western Carolina Teachers College, *Cullowhee, North Carolina*
Wisconsin State College Library, *Milwaukee, Wisconsin*

❈ IV ❈

Akron Public Library, *Akron, Ohio* (A. Polsky and
    Company, *Akron, Ohio*)

Alderman Library, University of Virginia,
    Charlottesville, Virginia (Paul Mellon)

American University, *Washington, D.C.*

Austin College, *Sherman, Texas*

Barnard College, *New York, New York*

Belhaven College, *Jackson, Mississippi* (Robert D.
    Sanders Foundation)

Berea College, *Berea, Kentucky* (Henry R. Levy)

Berkeley Public Library, *Berkeley, California* (Great
    Books Discussion Leaders, *Berkeley, California*)

Beverly Hills Public Library, *Beverly Hills, California*
    (Mrs. Arthur E. English)

Bryn Mawr College, *Bryn Mawr, Pennsylvania* (Mr. and
    Mrs. Henry A. Loeb)

Carleton College, *Northfield, Minnesota* (John Cowles)

Carnegie Institute Library, *Pittsburgh, Pennsylvania*
    (Charles J. Rosenbloom)

Case Institute of Technology, *Cleveland, Ohio* (Frederic
    M. Bosworth)

Catholic University, *Washington, D.C.*

Centre College, *Danville Kentucky* (Elbert Gary
   Sutcliffe)

Chamberlain-Hunt Academy, *Port Gibson, Mississippi*
   (Robert D. Sanders Foundation)

The Choate School, *Wallingford, Connecticut* (Paul
   Mellon)

The Clayton Library, *Clayton, Missouri* (J. Lionberger
   Davis)

Cleveland College, Western Reserve University,
   Cleveland, Ohio (G. T. Howson and J. H.
   Michener)

Cleveland Public Library, *Cleveland, Ohio* (Sterling-
   Lindner-Davis Company, *Cleveland, Ohio*)

Coe College, *Cedar Rapids, Iowa*

College of Idaho, *Caldwell, Idaho* (C. C. Anderson
   Company, *Boise, Idaho*)

College of Puget Sound, *Tacoma, Washington* (The
   Bon Marché, *Tacoma, Washington*)

The College of St. Joseph on the Rio Grande,
   Albuquerque, New Mexico (Clinton P. Anderson)

Columbia College, Columbia University, *New York,
   New York* (Harold F. Linder)

Dallas Public Library, *Dallas, Texas* (Mr. and Mrs. J.
   Leddy Jones)

Dartmouth College, *Hanover, New Hampshire*
   (Harold F. Linder)

Deering Library, Northwestern University, *Evanston, Illinois*

DeGolyer Collection, University of Oklahoma Library, *Norman, Oklahoma* (E. DeGolyer)

DePaul University, *Chicago, Illinois* (Britton I. Budd)

District of Columbia Public Libraries, *Washington, D.C.*

Drury College, *Springfield, Missouri* (Heer's, Inc., *Springfield, Missouri*)

Everett Public Library, *Everett, Washington* (The Bon Marché, *Everett, Washington*)

Fisk University, *Nashville, Tennessee* (George T. Keating)

Foxcroft School, *Middleburg, Virginia* (Paul Mellon)

Franklin and Marshall College, *Lancaster, Pennsylvania* (Isaac D. Levy)

George F. Baker Trust, *New York New York* (George F. Baker, Jr.)

Georgetown University, *Washington, D.C.*

George Washington University, *Washington, D.C.*

Gilmour Academy, *Gates Mills, Ohio* (Charles M. Grace)

Goshen College, *Goshen, Indiana* (Mr. and Mrs. W. T. Stalter)

Graduate School of Public Health Library, University of Pittsburgh, *Pittsburgh, Pennsylvania* (Thomas Parran, M.D.)

Grand Rapids Public Library, *Grand Rapids, Michigan*
(Herpolsheimer Company, *Grand Rapids,
Michigan*)

Great Falls Public Library, *Great Falls, Montana*
(The Paris of Montana, *Great Falls, Montana*)

Greensboro Public Library, *Greensboro, North Carolina*
(The Meyer's Company, *Greensboro,
North Carolina*)

Greensburg Library Association, *Greensburg, Pennsylvania*
(A. E. Troutman Company, *Greensburg,
Pennsylvania*)

The Hackley Public Library, *Muskegon, Michigan*
(Hardy-Herpolsheimer Company, *Muskegon,
Michigan*)

Harpur College, *Endicott, New York* (Carleton A.
Cleveland)

Harvey Memorial Library, Moravian College,
Bethlehem, Pennsylvania (Mr. and Mrs. Clayton W.
Bernhardt)

The Hawthorne Library, *Berryville, Virginia* (Paul
Mellon)

Hazlehurst High School, *Hazlehurst, Mississippi*
(Robert D. Sanders Foundation)

Highland Park Public Library, *Highland Park, Illinois*
(Donald S. Trumbull)

Howard University, *Washington, D.C.* (Harold F. Linder)

Indiana County and Free Library, *Indiana, Pennsylvania* (A. E. Troutman Company *Indiana, Pennsylvania*)

Institute for Advanced Study, *Princeton, New Jersey* (Harold F. Linder)

International House, Columbia University, *New York, New York*

International House, University of California, *Berkeley, California*

International House, University of Chicago, *Chicago, Illinois*

Iowa Wesleyan College, *Mount Pleasant, Iowa* (Mr. and Mrs. George B. McKibbin)

Jackson Public Library, *Jackson, Michigan* (The L. H. Field Company, *Jackson, Michigan*)

Jewish Community Center, *Washington, D.C.*

Jewish Theological Seminary of America, *New York, New York* (Arthur L. H. Rubin)

Jewish Theological Seminary of America, *New York, New York* (Salomon Bros. & Hutzler)

John Hay Library, Brown University, *Providence, Rhode Island* (Harold H. Swift)

Knox College, *Galesburg Illinois* (H. J. Szold)

Lafayette College, *Easton, Pennsylvania* (Wm. Laubach & Sons, *Easton, Pennsylvania*)

Lake Charles Public Library, *Lake Charles, Louisiana* (The Muller Company, *Lake Charles, Louisiana*)

Lake Forest College, *Lake Forest, Illinois*

Lawrence College, *Appleton, Wisconsin* (D. C. Everest)

Lebanon Community Library, *Lebanon, Pennsylvania* (The Bon Ton, *Lebanon, Pennsylvania*)

Liberal Arts Foundation, *New York, New York* (Arthur L. H. Rubin)

Library of International Relations, *Chicago, Illinois* (Eunice F. Hale)

Lincoln Memorial University, *Harrogate, Tennessee* (Foreman M. Lebold)

Lower Columbia Junior College, *Longview, Washington* (The Bon Marché, *Longview, Washington*)

Madeira School, *Greenway, Fairfax County, Virginia*

Mary Armstrong Ayers Memorial, *Oak Park, Illinois* (Friends of the Oak Park Library, *Oak Park, Illinois*)

Maryville College, *Maryville, Tennessee* (Glen A. Lloyd)

Michigan State College, *East Lansing, Michigan* (Michigan National Bank, *Lansing, Michigan*)

Millsaps College, *Jackson, Mississippi* (Robert D. Sanders Foundation)

Mississippi Southern College, *Hattiesburg, Mississippi*
    (Robert D. Sanders Foundation)

Morehouse College, *Atlanta, Georgia* (Harry Scherman)

Mount Holyoke College, *South Hadley, Massachusetts*
    (Alfred K. Eddy)

New Mexico Military Institute, *Roswell, New Mexico*
    (A. Norman Into)

New Mexico School of Mines, *Socorro, New Mexico*
    (United States Potash Company, *New York,*
    New York)

New Mexico Western College, *Silver City, New Mexico*
    (Kennecott Copper Corporation, Chino Mines
    Division, *Hurley, New Mexico*)

The New York Public Library, *New York, New York*
    (Harold F. Linder)

Nicholas Murray Butler Library, Columbia University
    New York, New York (Willard V. King)

Northland College, *Ashland, Wisconsin* (D. C. Everest)

North Shore Congregation, Israel Library, *Glencoe,*
    Illinois (Mr. and Mrs. Louis H. Silver)

Osterhout Free Public Library, *Wilkes-Barre,*
    Pennsylvania (Pomeroy's Inc., *Wilkes-Barre,*
    Pennsylvania)

Paterson Free Public Library, *Paterson, New Jersey*
    (Quackenbush Company, *Paterson, New Jersey*)

Pennsylvania College for Women, *Pittsburgh,*
    Pennsylvania (Paul Mellon)

Pierson College, Yale University, *New Haven, Connecticut* (Harold F. Linder)

Piney Woods School, *Piney Woods, Mississippi* (Robert D. Sanders Foundation)

Pottsville Free Public Library, *Pottsville, Pennsylvania* (Pomeroy's Inc., *Pottsville, Pennsylvania*)

Princeton University, *Princeton, New Jersey* (Alfred T. Carton)

Rapid City Air Force Base, *Rapid City, South Dakota* (L. S. Donaldson Company, *Rapid City, South Dakota*)

Rockford College, *Rockford, Illinois* (Mrs. Tiffany Blake)

Roosevelt College, *Chicago, Illinois* (Robert Pollak)

St. Benedict's College, *Atchison, Kansas* (True E. Snowden)

St. John's College, *Annapolis, Maryland* (Paul Mellon)

St. Louis Public Library, *St. Louis, Missouri* (Friends of Charles H. Compton, *St. Louis, Missouri*)

Salt Lake City School Board, *Salt Lake City, Utah* (Geneva Steel Company, *Geneva, Utah*)

Saybrook College, Yale University, *New Haven, Connecticut* (Edison Dick)

Southwest Missouri State College, *Springfield, Missouri* (Heer's, Inc., *Springfield, Missouri*)

Southern Methodist University, *University Park, Texas* (The Titche-Goettinger Company, *Dallas, Texas*)

State College of Washington, *Pullman, Washington* (John W. Maloney, through Friends of the Library of the State College of Washington, *Pullman, Washington*)

Sterling Library, Yale University, *New Haven Connecticut* (Mr. and Mrs. Louis H. Silver)

Swarthmore College, *Swarthmore, Pennsylvania* (Harold F. Linder)

Syracuse Public Library, *Syracuse, New York* (Dey Bros. & Company, *Syracuse, New York*)

Trinity College Library, *Hartford, Connecticut* (Paul Mellon)

Trinity University, *San Antonio, Texas* (Joske's of Texas, *San Antonio, Texas*)

United States Naval Academy, *Annapolis, Maryland* (Harold F. Linder)

University of California, *Berkeley, California*

University of California at Los Angeles, *Los Angeles, California*

University of Chicago, *Chicago, Illinois* (Mr. and Mrs. Renslow P. Sherer)

University of Chicago Library, *Chicago, Illinois*

University of Cincinnati, *Cincinnati, Ohio* (The Rollman & Sons Company, *Cincinnati, Ohio*)

University of Iowa, *Iowa City, Iowa* (Henry Carlton Shull)

University of Maryland, *College Park, Maryland*

University of New Mexico, *Albuquerque, New Mexico* (Potash Company of America, *Carlsbad, New Mexico*)

University of Tampa, *Tampa, Florida* (Maas Bros., *Tampa, Florida*)

University of Virginia, *Charlottesville, Virginia*

University of Virginia, *Charlottesville, Virginia* (Paul Mellon)

Valeria Home, Inc., *Oscawana, New York* (John Langeloth Loeb)

Varnum Memorial Library, *Jeffersonville, Vermont* (Scott Buchanan)

Virginia Military Institute, *Lexington, Virginia* (R. C. Kramer)

Virginia Polytechnical Institute, *Blacksburg, Virginia* (Paul Mellon)

Wabash College, *Crawfordsville, Indiana* (Pierre F. Goodrich)

Warren Library Association, *Warren, Pennsylvania* (Metzger-Wright Company, *Warren, Pennsylvania*)

Weber College, *Ogden, Utah* (C. C. Anderson Company, *Ogden, Utah*)

Wharton County High School, *Wharton, Texas* (Mrs. Clive Runnells)

Whitman College, *Walla Walla, Washington* (The Bon Marché, *Walla Walla, Washington*)

Whitworth College, *Spokane, Washington* (The Bon Marché, *Spokane, Washington*)

Wilson College, *Chambersburg, Pennsylvania* (Mrs. Thomas A. Mellon)

Winchester Foundation, *Winchester, Indiana* (Pierre F. Goodrich)

Woodland High School, *Woodland, California*

Yakima Valley Junior College, *Yakima, Washington* (Barnes-Woodin Company, *Yakima, Washington*)

Yale University, *New Haven, Connecticut*

Young Men's and Young Women's Hebrew Association, *New York, New York* (John Langeloth Loeb)

Other Institutions or Organizations

Chicago Lying-In Hospital, *Chicago, Illinois* (Claire D. Swift)

Commonwealth Edison Company Library, *Chicago, Illinois* (Charles Y. Freeman)

Minneapolis Star & Tribune Library, *Minneapolis Minnesota* (John Cowles)

The Washington Post Library, *Washington, D.C.*

GUIDE TO THIS SET

1. The list of authors
   See front end-papers in each volume

2. The list of the great ideas
   See rear end-papers in each volume

3. Explanation of colors of bindings
   See Volume 1, p. 86

4. Biography of each author
   See the Biographical Note preceding each author's work

5. Explanation of history and structure of this set
   See Volume 1, pp. xi-xxvii

6. Statement of the purpose of this set
   See Volume 1, pp. 1–82

7. Possible approaches to the reading of this set
   See Volume 1, pp. 85–89

8. Complete list of works included in this set
   See Volume 1, pp. 93–110

9. Suggested ten-year reading plan
   See Volume 1, pp. 112–131

10. Explanation of purpose, structure and use of *The Great Ideas, A Syntopicon of Great Books of the Western World* (Volumes 2 and 3)
    See Volume 1, pp. xxv–xxvi; and Volume 2, pp. xi–xxxi

11. General contents of the *Syntopicon*
    See Volume 2, p. vii; Volume 3, p. v

12. History of the *Syntopicon* and the principles and methods of its construction
    See Volume 3, pp. 1219–1299

GUIDE TO THIS SET

13. Additional readings suggested under the head of each of the 102 great ideas
    See the end of each chapter of the Syntopicon

14. Information about the 1,181 authors and 2,603 titles cited in the 102 reading lists
    See the Bibliography of Additional Readings (Volume 3, pp. 1143–1217)

15. Alphabetical list of 1,792 ideas, concepts, and terms dealt with under the 2,987 topics of the *Syntopicon*
    See the Inventory of Terms (Volume 3, pp. 1303–1345)

16. List of page locations of the Outlines of Topics for each of the 102 great ideas
    See Volume 3, p. 1346

CONTENTS

Preface: The History and Purpose of This Set   xi

The Great Conversation

    I. The Tradition of the West   1

   II. Modern Times   7

  III. Education and Economics   17

  IV. The Disappearance of Liberal Education   24

   V. Experimental Science   32

  VI. Education for All   42

 VII. The Education of Adults   52

VIII. The Next Great Change   57

  IX. East and West   66

   X. A Letter to the Reader   74

Possible Approaches to This Set   85

   I: The Contents of This Set   93

  II: Ten Years of Reading in This Set   112

✕ PREFACE ✕

✕ UNTIL lately the West has regarded it as self-evident that the road to education lay through great books. No man was educated unless he was acquainted with the masterpieces of his tradition. There never was very much doubt in anybody's mind about which the masterpieces were. They were the books that had endured and that the common voice of mankind called the finest creations, in writing, of the Western mind.

In the course of history, from epoch to epoch, new books have been written that have won their place in the list. Books once thought entitled to belong to it have been superseded; and this process of change will continue as long as men can think and write. It is the task of every generation to reassess the tradition in which it lives, to discard what it cannot use, and to bring into context with the distant and intermediate past the most recent contributions to the Great Conversation. This set of books is the result of an attempt to reappraise and re-embody the tradition of the West for our generation.

THE GREAT CONVERSATION

The Editors do not believe that any of the social and political changes that have taken place in the last fifty years, or any that now seem imminent, have invalidated or can invalidate the tradition or make it irrelevant for modern men. On the contrary, they are convinced that the West needs to recapture and re-emphasize and bring to bear upon its present problems the wisdom that lies in the works of its greatest thinkers and in the discussion that they have carried on.

This set of books is offered in no antiquarian spirit. We have not seen our task as that of taking tourists on a visit to ancient ruins or to the quaint productions of primitive peoples. We have not thought of providing our readers with hours of relaxation or with an escape from the dreadful cares that are the lot of every man in the second half of the twentieth century after Christ. We are as concerned as anybody else at the headlong plunge into the abyss that Western civilization seems to be taking. We believe that the voices that may recall the West to sanity are those which have taken part in the Great Conversation. We want them to be heard again—not because we want to go back to antiquity, or the Middle Ages, or the Renaissance, or the Eighteenth Century. We are quite aware that we do not live in any time but the present, and, distressing as the present is, we would not care to live in any other time if we could. We want the voices of the Great Conversation to be heard again because we think they may help us to learn to live better now.

We believe that in the passage of time the neglect of these books in the twentieth century will be regarded as an aberration, and not, as it is sometimes called today, a sign of progress. We think that progress, and progress in education in particular, depends on the incorporation of the ideas and images included in this set in the daily lives of all of us, from childhood through old age. In this view the disappearance of great books from education and from the reading of adults constitutes a calamity. In this view education in the West has been steadily deteriorating; the rising generation has been deprived of its birthright; the mess of pottage it has received in exchange has not been nutritious; adults have come to lead lives comparatively rich in material comforts and very poor in moral, intellectual, and spiritual tone.

We do not think that these books will solve all our problems. We do not think that they are the only books worth reading. We think that these books shed some light on all our basic problems, and that it is folly to do without any light we can get. We think that these books show the origins of many of our most serious difficulties. We think that the spirit they represent and the habit of mind they teach are more necessary today than ever before. We think that the reader who does his best to understand these books will find himself led to read and helped to understand other books. We think that reading and understanding great books will give him a standard by which to judge all other books.

[margin note: Value of the Great Books]

We believe that the reduction of the citizen to an object of propaganda, private and public, is one of the greatest dangers to democracy. A prevalent notion is that the great mass of the people cannot understand and cannot form an independent judgment upon any matter; they cannot be educated, in the sense of developing their intellectual powers, but they can be bamboozled. The reiteration of slogans, the distortion of the news, the great storm of propaganda that beats upon the citizen twenty-four hours a day all his life long mean either that democracy must fall a prey to the loudest and most persistent propagandists or that the people must save themselves by strengthening their minds so that they can appraise the issues for themselves.

Great books alone will not do the trick; for the people must have the information on which to base a judgment as well as the ability to make one. In order to understand infla-

[margin note: Also need reliable info]

tion, for example, and to have an intelligent opinion as to what can be done about it, the economic facts in a given country at a given time have to be available. Great books cannot help us there. But they can help us to that grasp of history, politics, morals, and economics and to that habit of mind which are needed to form a valid judgment on the issue. Great books may even help us to know what information we should demand. If we knew what information to demand we might have a better chance of getting it.

Though we do not recommend great books as a panacea for our ills, we must admit that we have an exceedingly high opinion of them as an educational instrument. We think of them as the best educational instrument for young people and adults today. By this we do not mean that this particular set is the last word that can be said on the subject. We may have made errors of selection. We hope that this collection may some day be revised in the light of the criticism it will receive. But the idea that liberal education is the education that everybody ought to have, and that the best way to a liberal education in the West is through the greatest works the West has produced, is still, in our view, the best educational idea there is.

The elements of novelty in the present-day presentation of this idea are accounted for by the changes of the past fifty years. For reasons that will be later described, great books have disappeared, or almost disappeared, from American education. Since we take American education as the prototype of education in any highly developed industrial democracy, we predict their disappearance everywhere in the West. As I have said, we regard this disappearance as an aberration, and not as an indication of progress. We do not look upon this disappearance as a benefit to be thankful for, but as an error that should be corrected. The element of novelty that results from

PREFACE

the disappearance of the books we take to be novelty only in the most superficial sense. We see this set as continuing a tradition that has been only momentarily interrupted.

A second element of novelty in the presentation of these books at this time is found in the proposition that democracy requires liberal education for all. We believe that this proposition is true. We concede that it has not been "scientifically" proved. We call upon our fellow citizens to test it. We think they will agree that, if this is the ideal, we should struggle to reach it and not content ourselves with inferior substitutes until we are satisfied that the goal cannot be attained.

The third element of novelty in the effort to restore these books to education is found in the conception of adult education that we wish to advance. Until very recently the education of adults the world over was regarded as compensatory; opportunity for adult study was offered those whose economic, social, or political position had deprived them, in ways often regarded as unjust, of the amount of formal education usual among the "superior" classes.

I am referring here, of course, only to general nonvocational education. Many other kinds of educational activities for adults have traveled under other banners: labor unions have wanted to train their members in industrial bargaining; individuals have wanted to prepare themselves for better jobs. When a man had made up for the deficiencies of his formal schooling, his obligation, and usually his desire, to educate himself naturally disappeared. He had reached the goal he had set for himself. I think it fair to say that in most countries of the world today the notion that a man who had "had" in childhood and youth the best institutional education the country had to offer should go on educating himself all his life would be regarded as fantastic.

Yet we believe that the obligation rests on all of us, uneducated, miseducated, and educated alike, to do just that. We do not depreciate the possibilities of these books as a means of educating young people. We think the sooner the young are introduced to the Great Conversation the better. They will not be able to understand it very well; but they should be introduced to it in the hope that they will continue to take part in it and eventually understand it. But we confess that we have had principally in mind the needs of the adult population, who, in America at least, have as a result of the changes of the last fifty years the leisure to become educated men and women. They now have the chance to understand themselves through understanding their tradition. Our principal aim in putting these books together was to offer them the means of doing so.

The members of the Advisory Board, in addition to long experience as teachers of young people, had all devoted a large part of their lives to the education of adults. They had all sought to use great books for the purpose of educating adults. They determined to try to offer the means of liberal education in a coherent program. This set of books was the result.

The Board asked itself whether an individual book contributed in an important way to the Great Conversation. The members drew upon their experience in teaching as a guide. They do not claim that all the great books of the West are here. They would not be embarrassed at the suggestion that they had omitted a book, or several books, greater than any they had included. They would be disturbed if they thought they had omitted books essential to a liberal education or had included any that had little bearing upon it.

The discussions of the Board revealed few differences of opinion about the overwhelming majority of the books in the list. The set is almost self-selected, in the sense that one book leads to another, amplifying, modifying, or contradicting it.

PREFACE

There is not much doubt about which are the most important voices in the Great Conversation. Of marginal cases there are a few. Many readers will be disappointed to find one, at least, of their favorite works missing. Many readers will be surprised to find some author of whom they had a low opinion given a place of honor. The final decision on the list was made by me. I do not pretend that my prejudices played no part; I would like to claim that I sought, obtained, and usually accepted excellent advice.

Readers who are startled to find the Bible omitted from the set will be reassured to learn that this was done only because Bibles are already widely distributed, and it was felt unnecessary to bring another, by way of this set, into homes that had several already. References to the Bible are, however, included in both the King James and the Douai versions under the appropriate topics in the *Syntopicon*.

The Editors felt that the chronological order was the most appropriate organizing principle for the volumes of this set. Since they conceived of this collection of books as reproducing a conversation among its authors, it was a natural decision to make the successive volumes of the set present, so far as possible, the authors in the temporal sequence in which they took part in that conversation.

Examining the chronological structure of the set, the reader will also note that the Great Conversation covers more than twenty-five centuries. But he may wonder at its apparent termination with the end of the nineteenth century. With the exception of some of Freud's writings, all the other works here assembled were written or published before 1900; and some of Freud's important works were published before that date.

The Editors do not think that the Great Conversation came to an end before the twentieth century began. On the contrary, they know that the Great Conversation has been going on during the first half of this century, and they hope it will continue to go on during the rest of this century and the centuries to follow. They are confident that great books have been written since 1900 and that the twentieth century will contribute many new voices to the Great Conversation.

The reason, then, for the omission of authors and works after 1900 is simply that the Editors did not feel that they or anyone else could accurately judge the merits of contemporary writings. During the editorial deliberations about the contents of the set, more difficult problems were encountered in the case of nineteenth-century authors and titles than with regard to those of any preceding century. The cause of these difficulties—the proximity of these authors and works to our own day and our consequent lack of perspective with regard to them—would make it far more difficult to make a selection of twentieth-century authors. If the reader is interested in knowing some of the possible candidates for inclusion from the twentieth century, he will find their names in the Bibliography of Additional Readings, which is appended to the *Syntopicon* (in Volume 3, pp. 1143-1217). The Additional Readings that come at the end of each of the *Syntopicon's* 102 chapters on the great ideas try to make an adequate representation of works written in this century; and in doing so, they name books that may prove themselves great, as other great books have done, by submission with the passage of time to the general judgment of mankind.

The Editors did not seek to assemble a set of books representative of various periods or countries. Antiquity and the Middle Ages, the Renaissance and modern times, are included in proportion as the great writers of these epochs contributed to the deepening, extension, or enrichment of the tradition of the West. It is worth noting that, though the period from 1500 to 1900 represents less than one-sixth of the total extent of the literary record of the Western tradition, the last four hundred years is represented in this set by more than one-half the volumes of *Great Books of the Western World*.

The Editors did not, in short, allot a certain space to a certain epoch in terms of the amount of time in human history that it consumed. Nor did we arbitrarily allot a certain space to a certain country. We tried to find the most important voices in the Conversation, without regard to the language they spoke. We did encounter some difficulties with language that we thought insurmountable. Where the excellence of a book depended principally on the excellence of its language, and where no adequate translation could be found or made, we were constrained reluctantly to omit it.

We thought it no part of our duty to emphasize national contributions, even those of our own country. I omitted Emerson, Whitman, Thoreau, and Mark Twain, all very great writers, because I felt that, important as they were, they did not measure up to the other books in the set. They carried forward the Great Conversation, but not in such a way as to be indispensable to the comprehension of it. Obviously in a set made up of a limited number of volumes only the writers that seemed indispensable could be included.

Some writers have made an important contribution to the Great Conversation, but in a way that makes it impossible to include it in a set like this. These are writers, of whom Leibnitz, Voltaire, and Balzac are notable examples, whose contribution lies in the total volume of their work, rather than in a few great works, and whose total volume is too large to be included or whose single works do not come up to the standard of the other books in this set.

What we wanted first of all, of course, was to make these books available. In many cases, all or some of an author's works included in this set were unavailable. They were either inaccessible or prohibitively expensive. This is true of works by Aristotle, Galen, Euclid, Archimedes, Apollonius, Nicomachus, Ptolemy, Copernicus, Kepler, Plotinus, Aquinas, Gilbert, Harvey, Descartes, Pascal, Newton, Kant, Lavoisier, Fourier, Faraday, and Freud.

We attach importance to making whole works, as distinguished from excerpts, available; and in all but three cases, Aquinas, Kepler, and Fourier, the 443 works of the 74 authors in this set are printed complete. One of the policies upon which the Advisory Board insisted most strongly was that the great writers should be allowed to speak for themselves. They should speak with their full voice and not be digested or mutilated by editorial decisions. Undoubtedly this policy makes reading more difficult; for the reader becomes to this extent his own editor. No one will deny that many arid stretches are contained in the works of the great writers. But we believed that it would be presumptuous for us to do the reader's skipping for him. When Hermann Hesse referred to the present as "the Age of the Digest," he did not intend to say anything complimentary.

Since the set was conceived of as a great conversation, it is obvious that the books could not have been chosen with any dogma or even with any point of view in mind. In a conversation that has gone on for twenty-five centuries, all dogmas and points of view appear. Here are the great errors as well as the great truths. The reader has to determine which are the errors and which the truths. The task of interpretation and conclusion is his. This is the machinery and life of the Western tradition in the hands of free men.

The title of this set is *Great Books of the Western World*. I shall have more to say later about great books of the Eastern world and merely wish to remark here that in omitting them from this collection we do not intend to depreciate them. The conversation presented in this set is peculiar to the West. We believe that everybody, Westerners and Easterners, should understand it, not because it is better than anything the East can show, but because it is important to understand the West. We hope that editors who understand the tradition of the East will do for that part of the world what we have attempted for our own tradition in *Great Books of the Western World* and the *Syntopicon*. With that task accomplished for both the West and the East, it should be possible to put together the common elements in the traditions and to present Great Books of the World. Few things could do as much to advance the unity of mankind.

Some readers may feel that we have been too hard on them in insisting that the great works of science are a part of the conversation and that a man who has not read them has not acquired a liberal education. Others, who concede the importance of science to understanding the world today, may raise the question of whether it is possible to understand modern science and its contribution to the modern world through the medium of books of the past. They may feel that, whereas philosophy, history, and literature can produce works that are always fresh and new, natural science is progressive and is rapidly outdated. Why read Copernicus or Faraday if scientists now know everything that they knew, and much more besides?

It is interesting to note that, some years after the books had been selected for this set, President James B. Conant of Harvard, a distinguished chemist, proposed to make the kind of books selected central in a reform of scientific education for the layman. He said: "What I propose is the establishment of one or more courses at the college level on the Tactics and Strategy of Science. The objective would be to give a greater degree of understanding of science by the close study of a relatively few historical examples of the development of science. I suggest courses at the college level, for I do not believe they could be understood earlier in a student's educa-

xxi

tion; but there is no reason why they could not become important parts of programs of adult education. Indeed such courses might well prove particularly suitable for older groups of men and women. . . . The greatest hindrance to the widespread use of case histories in teaching science is the lack of suitable case material. . . . I am hopeful that if a sufficient number of teachers become interested in the approach suggested in the following pages a co-operative enterprise might be launched which would go far to overcome the difficulties now presented by the paucity of printed material available for student use. . . . Together they might plan for the translation, editing, and publishing in suitable form of extracts from the history of science which would be of importance to the college teacher. It is no small undertaking, but one of the first importance. When it is remembered that two of the most significant works in the history of science, the *De Revolutionibus* of Copernicus and the *De Fabrica* of Vesalius, have never been published in English translation—to say nothing of the vast amount of untranslated writings of Kepler, Galileo, Lavoisier, Galvani, and a host of others—it is evident how much remains to be accomplished."

The *De Revolutionibus* of Copernicus and writings of Kepler, Galileo, and Lavoisier appear in this set. So also do the mathematical and scientific works of nineteen others—Aristotle, Hippocrates, Galen, Euclid, Archimedes, Apollonius, Nicomachus, Ptolemy, Gilbert, Harvey, Descartes, Pascal, Newton, Huygens, Fourier, Faraday, Darwin, James, and Freud.

It is true that scientific works are often omitted from lists of important books on the assumption that such works lack the educational significance of the great poems, the great histories, and the great philosophies and are somehow not part of our "culture"; or that they cannot be read except by a few specialists; or that science, unlike poetry, has somehow "ad-

What's included re. science

vanced" in modern times in such fashion as to rob the great steps in that advance of any but antiquarian value.

But the Editors do not agree that the great poets of every time are to be walked with and talked with, but not those who brought deep insight into the mystery of number and magnitude or the natural phenomena they observed about them.

We do not agree that better means of observation or more precise instruments of measurement invalidate the thinking of great scientists of the past, even where such means cause us to correct the hypotheses of these scientists.

We lament the man who, properly desiring to wrestle at first hand with the problems that the great poets and philosophers have raised, yet contents himself with the "results" and "findings" of modern science.

We believe that it is a gratuitous assumption that anybody can read poetry but very few can read mathematics. In view of the countless engineers and technicians in our society we should expect many of our readers to find the mathematical and scientific masterpieces more understandable than many other works. As Stringfellow Barr has said, the world is rapidly dividing into technicians who cannot tell the difference between a good poem and sentimental doggerel and "cultured" people who know nothing about electricity except that you push a button when you want it. In a society that is highly technological the sooner the citizens understand the basic ideas of mathematics and natural science the better.

Poor books in science deal with specialties that serve the technician and pride themselves on juggling jargon. But the best books get their power from the refinement and precise use of the common language. As far as the medium of communication is concerned, they are products of the most elegant literary style, saying precisely what is meant. Like literary books, they have beginnings, middles, and ends that move from familiar situations through complications to unravelings and recognitions. They sometimes end in the revelation of familiar mysteries.

The atmosphere we breathe today, because of the universal use of gadgets and machines, because the word "scientific" is employed in a magical sense, and because of the half-hidden technological fabric of our lives, is full of the images and myths of science. The minds of men are full of shadows and reflections of things that they cannot grasp. As Scott Buchanan has said, "Popular science has made every man his own quack; he needs some of the doctor's medicine."

Much of this is the result of the mystery that modern man has made of mathematics. It is supposed that the scientist or engineer can understand great scientific works because he understands mathematics, which nobody but a scientist or engineer can understand. This is the reason why a fairly continuous series of great books in mathematics is contained in this set. The Editors believe that mathematical truth will set us free from the superstitious awe that surrounds the scientific enterprise today.

The reader will be able to decide for himself whether the mathematical and scientific works should have been excluded from this set on the score of their difficulty for the ordinary reader by comparing the difficulty, for such a reader, of Dante's *Divine Comedy* and that most difficult of all scientific works, Newton's *Principia*. There is a cult of scholarship surrounding Dante's masterpiece that is almost as formidable as the cult of mathematics. Most of this work is in philology, metaphysics, and history. The ordinary reader, who has heard of this apparatus but never used it, is surprised to find that he understands Dante without it.

Both the cult of learning around Dante and the cult of ignorance around Newton are phenomena of the vicious specialization of scholarship. Much of the background of Dante

is in Euclid and in Ptolemy's astronomy; the structure of
both the poem and the world it describes is mathematical.
Almost all of Newton by his express intention is Euclidean
in its arithmetic as well as its geometry. Dante no more
delivers his whole message without benefit of some mathematics than does Newton. Both are enhanced by the presence
of the scientific voice in the conversation of which they are
parts.

The Advisory Board recommended that no scholarly apparatus should be included in the set. No "introductions" giving the Editors' views of the authors should appear. The
books should speak for themselves, and the reader should decide for himself. Great books contain their own aids to reading; that is one reason why they are great. Since we hold that
these works are intelligible to the ordinary man, we see no
reason to interpose ourselves or anybody else between the
author and the reader.

The *Syntopicon**, which began as an index and then turned
into a means of helping the reader find paths through the
books, has ended, in addition to making these contributions
as a tool for reference, research, and study, as a preliminary
summation of the issues around which the Great Conversation has revolved, together with indications of the course of
the debate at this moment. Once again, the *Syntopicon* argues
no case and presents no point of view. It will not interpret any
book to the reader; it will not tell him which author is right
and which wrong on any question. It simply supplies him
with suggestions as to how he may conveniently pursue the
study of any important topic through the range of Western
intellectual history. It shows him how to find what great

*For a more elaborate description of the structure and uses of the *Syntopicon*, see the Possible
Approaches to This Set in this volume (pp. 85–89) and the Preface to the *Syntopicon* (Vol.
II, pp. xi–xxxi).

men have had to say about the greatest issues and what is being said about these issues today.

But I would do less than justice to Mr. Adler's achievement if I left the matter there. The *Syntopicon* is, in addition to all this, and in addition to being a monument to the industry, devotion, and intelligence of Mr. Adler and his staff, a step forward in the thought of the West. It indicates where we are: where the agreements and disagreements lie; where the problems are; where the work has to be done. It thus helps to keep us from wasting our time through misunderstanding and points to the issues that must be attacked. When the history of the intellectual life of this century is written, the *Syntopicon* will be regarded as one of the landmarks in it.

The Editors must record their gratitude to the Advisory Board and to their Editorial Consultants in the British Empire.

The Advisory Board consisted of Stringfellow Barr, Professor of History in the University of Virginia, and formerly President of St. John's College in Annapolis, Maryland; Scott Buchanan, philosopher, and formerly Dean of St. John's College; John Erskine, novelist, and formerly Professor of English in Columbia University; Clarence Faust, President of the Fund for the Advancement of Education and formerly Dean of the Humanities and Sciences in Leland Stanford University; Alexander Meiklejohn, philosopher, and formerly Chairman of the School for Social Studies in San Francisco; Joseph Schwab, scientist, and Professor in the College of the University of Chicago; and Mark Van Doren, poet, and Professor of English in Columbia University.

The Editorial Consultants were A. F. B. Clark, Professor of French Literature in the University of British Columbia, Canada; F. L. Lucas, Fellow and Lecturer of King's College,

PREFACE

Cambridge, England; and Walter Murdoch, Professor of English Literature in the University of Western Australia.

The Editors would also express their gratitude to Rudolph Ruzicka, designer and typographer, who planned the format of this set of books and designed the typography of its individual works in the light of his reading of them.

The Editors wish especially to mention their debt to the late John Erskine, who over thirty years ago began the movement to reintroduce the study of great books into American education, and who labored long and arduously on the preparation of this set. Their other special obligation is to Senator William Benton, who as a member of a discussion group in Great Books proposed the publication of this collection, and who as Publisher and Chairman of the Board of *Encyclopædia Britannica* has followed and fostered it and finally brought it out.

ROBERT M. HUTCHINS

THE GREAT CONVERSATION

CHAPTER I

The Tradition of the West

❧ THE tradition of the West is embodied in the Great Conversation that began in the dawn of history and that continues to the present day. Whatever the merits of other civilizations in other respects, no civilization is like that of the West in this respect. No other civilization can claim that its defining characteristic is a dialogue of this sort. No dialogue in any other civilization can compare with that of the West in the number of great works of the mind that have contributed to this dialogue. The goal toward which Western society moves is the Civilization of the Dialogue. The spirit of Western civilization is the spirit of inquiry. Its dominant element is the *Logos*. Nothing is to remain undiscussed. Everybody is to speak his mind. No proposition is to be left unexamined. The exchange of ideas is held to be the path to the realization of the potentialities of the race.

At a time when the West is most often represented by its

I

friends as the source of that technology for which the whole
world yearns and by its enemies as the fountainhead of selfish-
ness and greed, it is worth remarking that, though both elements can be found in the Great Conversation, the Western
ideal is not one or the other strand in the Conversation, but
the Conversation itself. It would be an exaggeration to say
that Western civilization means these books. The exaggeration would lie in the omission of the plastic arts and music,
which have quite as important a part in Western civilization
as the great productions included in this set. But to the extent
to which books can present the idea of a civilization, the idea
of Western civilization is here presented.

These books are the means of understanding our society and
ourselves. They contain the great ideas that dominate us
without our knowing it. There is no comparable repository
of our tradition.

To put an end to the spirit of inquiry that has characterized
the West it is not necessary to burn the books. All we have to
do is to leave them unread for a few generations. On the other
hand, the revival of interest in these books from time to time
throughout history has provided the West with new drive
and creativeness. Great books have salvaged, preserved, and
transmitted the tradition on many occasions similar to our
own.

The books contain not merely the tradition, but also the
great exponents of the tradition. Their writings are models of
the fine and liberal arts. They hold before us what Whitehead
called "the habitual vision of greatness." These books have
endured because men in every era have been lifted beyond
themselves by the inspiration of their example. Sir Richard
Livingstone said: "We are tied down, all our days and for
the greater part of our days, to the commonplace. That is
where contact with great thinkers, great literature helps.
In their company we are still in the ordinary world, but

2

it is the ordinary world transfigured and seen through the eyes of wisdom and genius. And some of their vision becomes our own."

Until very recently these books have been central in education in the West. They were the principal instrument of liberal education, the education that men acquired as an end in itself, for no other purpose than that it would help them to be men, to lead human lives, and better lives than they would otherwise be able to lead.

The aim of liberal education is human excellence, both private and public (for man is a political animal). Its object is the excellence of man as man and man as citizen. It regards man as an end, not as a means; and it regards the ends of life, and not the means to it. For this reason it is the education of free men. Other types of education or training treat men as means to some other end, or are at best concerned with the means of life, with earning a living, and not with its ends.

The substance of liberal education appears to consist in the recognition of basic problems, in knowledge of distinctions and interrelations in subject matter, and in the comprehension of ideas.

Liberal education seeks to clarify the basic problems and to understand the way in which one problem bears upon another. It strives for a grasp of the methods by which solutions can be reached and the formulation of standards for testing solutions proposed. The liberally educated man understands, for example, the relation between the problem of the immortality of the soul and the problem of the best form of government; he understands that the one problem cannot be solved by the same method as the other, and that the test that he will have to bring to bear upon solutions proposed differs from one problem to the other.

The liberally educated man understands, by understanding the distinctions and interrelations of the basic fields of sub-

3

ject matter, the differences and connections between poetry and history, science and philosophy, theoretical and practical science; he understands that the same methods cannot be applied in all these fields; he knows the methods appropriate to each.

The liberally educated man comprehends the ideas that are relevant to the basic problems and that operate in the basic fields of subject matter. He knows what is meant by soul, state, God, beauty, and by the other terms that are basic to the discussion of fundamental issues. He has some notion of the insights that these ideas, singly or in combination, provide concerning human experience.

The liberally educated man has a mind that can operate well in all fields. He may be a specialist in one field. But he can understand anything important that is said in any field and can see and use the light that it sheds upon his own. The liberally educated man is at home in the world of ideas and in the world of practical affairs, too, because he understands the relation of the two. He may not be at home in the world of practical affairs in the sense of liking the life he finds about him; but he will be at home in that world in the sense that he understands it. He may even derive from his liberal education some conception of the difference between a bad world and a good one and some notion of the ways in which one might be turned into the other.

The method of liberal education is the liberal arts, and the result of liberal education is discipline in those arts. The liberal artist learns to read, write, speak, listen, understand, and think. He learns to reckon, measure, and manipulate matter, quantity, and motion in order to predict, produce, and exchange. As we live in the tradition, whether we know it or not, so we are all liberal artists, whether we know it or not. We all practice the liberal arts, well or badly, all the time every day. As we should understand the tradition as well as we can in order to understand ourselves, so we should be as good liberal artists as we can in order to become as fully human as we can.

The liberal arts are not merely indispensable; they are unavoidable. Nobody can decide for himself whether he is going to be a human being. The only question open to him is whether he will be an ignorant, undeveloped one or one who has sought to reach the highest point he is capable of attaining. The question, in short, is whether he will be a poor liberal artist or a good one.

The tradition of the West in education is the tradition of the liberal arts. Until very recently nobody took seriously the suggestion that there could be any other ideal. The educational ideas of John Locke, for example, which were directed to the preparation of the pupil to fit conveniently into the social and economic environment in which he found himself, made no impression on Locke's contemporaries. And so it will be found that other voices raised in criticism of liberal education fell upon deaf ears until about a half-century ago.

This Western devotion to the liberal arts and liberal education must have been largely responsible for the emergence of democracy as an ideal. The democratic ideal is equal opportunity for full human development, and, since the liberal arts are the basic means of such development, devotion to democracy naturally results from devotion to them. On the other hand, if acquisition of the liberal arts is an intrinsic part of human dignity, then the democratic ideal demands that we should strive to see to it that all have the opportunity to attain to the fullest measure of the liberal arts that is possible --to each.

The present crisis in the world has been precipitated by the vision of the range of practical and productive art offered by the West. All over the world men are on the move, expressing their determination to share in the technology in which the

West has excelled. This movement is one of the most spectacular in history, and everybody is agreed upon one thing about it: we do not know how to deal with it. It would be tragic if in our preoccupation with the crisis we failed to hold up as a thing of value for the world, even as that which might show us a way in which to deal with the crisis, our vision of the best that the West has to offer. That vision is the range of the liberal arts and liberal education. Our determination about the distribution of the fullest measure of these arts and this education will measure our loyalty to the best in our own past and our total service to the future of the world.

The great books were written by the greatest liberal artists. They exhibit the range of the liberal arts. The authors were also the greatest teachers. They taught one another. They taught all previous generations, up to a few years ago. The question is whether they can teach us. To this question we now turn.

6

Modern Times

X Until recently great books were central in liberal education; but liberal education was limited to an élite. So great books were limited to an élite and to those few of the submerged classes who succeeded in breaking into them in spite of the barriers that society threw up around them. Where anybody bothered to defend this exclusion, it was done on the basis that only those with exceptional intelligence and leisure could understand these books, and that only those who had political power needed to understand them.

As the masses were admitted to political activity, it was assumed that, though they must be educated, they could not be educated in this way. They had to learn to read the newspaper and to write a business letter and to make change; but how could they be expected to study Plato or Dante or Newton? All that they needed to know about great writers could

[handwritten margin notes: Great books/ lib ed only for élites in past]

[handwritten margin notes: Now educating masses. Assumed lib ed too hard]

be translated for them in textbooks that did not suffer from the embarrassment of being either difficult or great.

The people now have political power and leisure. If they have not always used them wisely, it may be because they have not had the kind of education that would enable them to do so.

It is not argued that education through great books and the liberal arts was a poor education for the élite. It is argued that times have changed and that such an education would be a poor education for anybody today, since it is outmoded. It is remote from real life and today's problems. Many of the books were written when men held slaves. Many were written in a prescientific and preindustrial age. What can they have to say to us, free, democratic citizens of a scientific, industrial era?

This is a kind of sociological determinism. As economic determinism holds that all activity is guided and regulated by the conditions of production, so sociological determinism claims that intellectual activity, at least, is always relative to a particular society, so that, if the society changes in an important way, the activity becomes irrelevant. Ideas originating in one state of society can have no bearing on another state of society. If they seem to have a bearing, this is only seeming. Ideas are the rationalizations of the social conditions that exist at any given time. If we seek to use in our own time the ideas of another, we shall deceive ourselves, because by definition these ideas have no application to any other time than that which produced them.

History and common sense explode sociological determinism, and economic determinism, too. There is something called man on this earth. He wrestles with his problems and tries to solve them. These problems change from epoch to epoch in certain respects; they remain the same in others. What is the good life? What is a good state? Is there a God?

8

What is the nature and destiny of man? Such questions and a host of others persist because man persists, and they will persist as long as he does. Through the ages great men have written down their discussion of these persistent questions. Are we to disdain the light they offer us on the ground that they lived in primitive, far-off times? As someone has remarked, "The Greeks could not broadcast the Aeschylean tragedy; but they could write it."

This set of books explodes sociological determinism, because it shows that no age speaks with a single voice. No society so determines intellectual activity that there can be no major intellectual disagreements in it. The conservative and the radical, the practical man and the theoretician, the idealist and the realist will be found in every society, many of them conducting the same kind of arguments that are carried on today. Although man has progressed in many spectacular respects, I suppose it will not be denied that he is today worse off in many respects, some of them more important than the respects in which he has improved. We should not reject the help of the sages of former times. We need all the help we can get.

The chief exponent of the view that times have changed and that our conception of the best education must change with them is that most misunderstood of all philosophers of education, John Dewey. It is one of the ironies of fate that his followers who have misunderstood him have carried all before them in American education; whereas the plans he proposed have never been tried. The notion that is perhaps most popular in the United States, that the object of education is to adjust the young to their environment, and in particular to teach them to make a living, John Dewey roundly condemned; yet it is usually advanced in his name.

Dewey was first of all a social reformer. He could not advocate adjustment to an environment the brutality and injustice

9

of which repelled him. He believed in his own conception of liberal education for all and looked upon any kind of training directed to learning a trade, solely to make a living at it, as narrowing and illiberal. He would especially repudiate those who seek to differentiate among the young on the basis of their capacity in order to say that only some are capable of acquiring a liberal education, in Dewey's conception of it or any other.

John Dewey's central position is stated in his major book on education, *Democracy and Education*, published in 1916. He says: "Both practically and philosophically, the key to the present educational situation lies in a gradual reconstruction of school materials and methods so as to utilize various forms of occupation typifying social callings, and to bring out their intellectual and moral content." The occupations that are to be engaged in are those "which are indicated by the needs and interests of the pupil at the time. Only in this way can there be on the part of the educator and of the one educated a genuine discovery of personal aptitudes so that the proper choice of a specialized pursuit in later life may be indicated. Moreover, the discovery of capacity and aptitude will be a *constant* progress as long as growth continues."

Dewey's chief reason for this recommendation is found in his psychology of learning. "An occupation is a continuous activity having a purpose. Education *through* occupations consequently combines within itself more of the factors conducive to learning than any other method. It calls instincts and habits into play; it is a foe to passive receptivity. It has an end in view; results are to be accomplished. Hence it appeals to thought; it demands that an idea of an end be steadily maintained, so that activity must be progressive, leading from one stage to another; observation and ingenuity are required at each stage to overcome obstacles and to discover and readjust means of execution. In short, an occupation, pursued under conditions where the realization of the activity rather than merely the external product is the aim, fulfills the requirements which were laid down earlier in connection with the discussion of aims, interest, and thinking."

The doctrine is that occupations, means of earning a living, should constitute the object of the attention of the educational system. This is not for the purpose of teaching the pupils how to make a living. Dewey opposes pure vocational training and urges that "a truly liberal, and liberating, education would refuse today to isolate vocational training on any of its levels from a continuous education in the social, moral and scientific contexts within which wisely administered callings and professions must function." He proposes education through occupations as a means of arousing interest, which it is assumed can be aroused by the study of occupations, of helping students to select a vocation, and of showing them the significance of the various ways of earning a living.

This is not the place for an elaborate critique of this doctrine. It is perhaps enough to say that the misinterpretations and misapplications of it were natural and inevitable. A program of social reform cannot be achieved through the educational system unless it is one that the society is prepared to accept. The educational system is the society's attempt to perpetuate itself and its own ideals. If a society wishes to improve, it will use the educational system for that purpose. Even in this case it will not allow the educational system to determine for itself what improvement is, unless it is a society that believes that the free and independent exercise of individual judgment is the best way to achieve improvement. If a society does not wish to change, it cannot be reformed through the educational system. In practice, a program of social reform will turn out to be what Dewey's has turned out to be in the hands of his followers, a program of social adjustment.

II

So a program of education *through* occupations will in practice turn out to be a program of education *for* occupations. Indeed, Dewey never tells us how it can be anything else. He does not say how he would accomplish the study of the moral, social, scientific, and intellectual contexts of occupations without resorting to those great books and those liberal arts which he regards as outmoded by experimental science and industrialization.

Dewey never says details

Nor does he indicate any awareness of the practical difficulties of having occupations studied at school. The school cannot duplicate the actual conditions of industry, commerce, finance, and the learned professions. Machines, methods, teachers can never be up to date. The conditions in the educational system generally can never be those that obtain in the modern medical school, in which the atmosphere of reality does not have to be created, because it is already there: the patient is really sick; the professor is trying to cure him; and the student learns to be a doctor by acting as the professor's assistant.

Impractical

Dewey is certainly correct in saying that the actual conditions of practice teach by arousing interest and defining the aim. But he fails to notice that this leads not to the study of occupations in the educational system, but to the study of occupations through apprenticeship. This is the situation in the medical school. The apprentice is committed to the occupation and learns it under the actual conditions of practice. In the educational system generally the actual conditions of practice cannot be successfully imitated; and the pupil is not committed to the occupation.

Since the pupil is not committed to the occupation, the proposition that the occupations that are to be studied are those which are indicated by the needs and interests of the pupil at the time is alarming. Between the ages of six and fourteen I wanted, in rapid succession, to be an iceman (a now

12

extinct occupation), a "motorman" on the horse cars (also extinct), a fireman, a postman, a policeman, a professional baseball player, and a missionary. The notion that what my teachers should have done was to offer me a study of these occupations as the fancy for each of them took me is so startling that Mr. Dewey's followers may perhaps be excused for refusing to take him literally and contenting themselves with trade-school instruction looking toward earning a living.

The educational results of studies of occupations as the passing whims of children suggested them would hardly be what Mr. Dewey hoped, even if such a curriculum could in fact be instituted, as it never has been. One educational proposition I take to be axiomatic, that matters that demand experience of those who seek to understand them cannot be understood by those who are without experience. A child can and should learn about the economic and political system by way of introduction to it, but he cannot understand it, in the same way or to the same degree that he can understand arithmetic, music, and science. Nor can he understand the moral and social contents of occupations in which he has never engaged under the actual conditions of practice.

As the quotations I have given show, Mr. Dewey wants to concentrate on the study of occupations because he thinks that they will arouse real interest and lead to real learning. But the interest of the young in occupations is neither intense nor permanent, except in the case of an individual with a very special, overwhelming bent, until the time is almost at hand at which they have to make up their minds about the choice of their careers. Even then they can learn little about them until they have engaged in them, as the apprentice does, under the conditions under which they are carried on in the world. They cannot understand them; least of all can they

13

understand their social and economic and political contexts, until they have had some experience as wage earners and citizens. I say again that imitation experiences in the classroom are not a substitute for actual experiences in life. Such experiences can lead only to illusion: they lead the pupil to think he understands something when he does not.

From the looks of things, all young Americans of a certain age now want to be cowboys. I doubt whether it would be useful for the schools to concentrate on cowpunching in its moral, social, political, scientific, and intellectual contexts. I do not see how the schools could do it, except by apprenticing the pupils to cowmen. I doubt whether, in the absence of such apprenticeship, much real learning would result. I doubt that, if it were possible to arouse real interest in cowmanship and its various contexts and to train up a generation of accomplished cowboys through the educational system, it would be in the public interest to dedicate the educational system to this purpose.

The reason is, apart from those I have already mentioned, that to regard the study of occupations as central in education assigns them a place to which they are not entitled. Work is for the sake of leisure. What will Mr. Dewey do about leisure? Will he ignore the end and concentrate on the means, so that, when the means have given us the end, we do not know what to do with ourselves? What about the duties of citizenship, which are more complicated and more important than at any time in history? Will the study of occupations, in all their contexts, help us to achieve that intellectual independence which democratic citizenship requires? Is it not a fact that we are now so wrapped up in our own occupations and the special interests of our own occupational groups that we are almost at the pretyrannical stage described by Vico, the stage where everybody is so concerned with his own special interests that nobody looks

14

after the common good? Is not the study of occupations the way to hasten the disintegration of such community as still remains, through emphasizing our individuality at the expense of our common humanity?

Democracy and Education was written before the assembly line had achieved its dominant position in the industrial world and before mechanization had depopulated the farms of America. The signs of these processes were already at hand; and Dewey saw the necessity of facing the social problems they would raise. One of these is the humanization of work. His book is a noble, generous effort to solve this and other social problems through the educational system. Unfortunately, the methods he proposed would not solve these problems; they would merely destroy the educational system.

The humanization of work is one of the most baffling issues of our time. We cannot hope to get rid of work altogether. We cannot say that we have dealt adequately with work when we have urged the prolongation of leisure.

Whatever work there is should have as much meaning as possible. Wherever possible, workmen should be artists; their work should be the application of knowledge or science and known and enjoyed by them as such. They should, if possible, know what they are doing, why what they are doing has the results it has, why they are doing it, and what constitutes the goodness of the things produced. They should understand what happens to what they produce, why it happens in that way, and how to improve what happens. They should understand their relations to others co-operating in a given process, the relation of that process to other processes, the pattern of them all as constituting the economy of the nation, and the bearing of the economy on the social, moral, and political life of the nation and the world. Work would be humanized if understanding of all these kinds were in it and around it.

To have these kinds of understanding the man who works

15

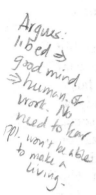

Argues:
libed ⇒
good mind
⇒ human. g
work. No
need to fear
ppl. won't be able
to make a
living.

must have a good mind. The purpose of education is to de-velop a good mind. Everybody should have equal access to the kind of education most likely to develop such a mind and should have it for as long as it takes to acquire enough intel-lectual excellence to fix once and for all the vision of the continuous need for more and more intellectual excellence.

This is the educational path to the humanization of work. The man who acquires some intellectual excellence and in-tends to go on acquiring more will, to borrow a phrase from Dewey, "reconstruct and reorganize his experience." We need have few fears that he will not be able to learn how to make a living. In addition to performing this indispensable task, he will inquire critically about the kind of life he leads while making a living. He will seek to understand the man-ner in which the life of all is affected by the way he and his fellow workers are making a living. He will develop all the meaning there is in his work and go on to see to it that it has more and better meaning.

This set of books is offered not merely as an object upon which leisure may be expended, but also as a means to the humanization of work through understanding.

✦ CHAPTER III ✦

Education and Economics

✦APART from John Dewey
and those few of his followers who understand him, most
writers on education hold that, though education through
great books and the liberal arts is still the best education for
the few, it cannot be the best education for the many, because
the many have not the capacity to acquire it.

It would seem that this education is the best for everybody,
if it is the best for the best, provided everybody can get it.
The question, then, is: Can everybody get it? This is the most
important question in education. Perhaps it is the most important question in the world.

Nobody knows the answer to this question. There has never
been a time in history when everybody has had a chance to
get a liberal education. We can, however, examine the alternatives, and the consequences of each.

If leisure and political power are a reason for liberal education, then everybody in America now has this reason, and everybody where democracy and industrialization penetrate will ultimately have it. If leisure and political power require this education, everybody in America now requires it, and everybody where democracy and industrialization penetrate will ultimately require it. If the people are not capable of acquiring this education, they should be deprived of political power and probably of leisure. Their uneducated political power is dangerous, and their uneducated leisure is degrading and will be dangerous. If the people are incapable of achieving the education that responsible democratic citizenship demands, then democracy is doomed, Aristotle rightly condemned the mass of mankind to natural slavery, and the sooner we set about reversing the trend toward democracy the better it will be for the world.

On the other hand, the conclusion that everybody should have the chance to have that education which will fit him for responsible democratic citizenship and which will develop his human powers to the fullest degree does not require the immediate adoption in any given country of universal liberal education. This conclusion states the ideal toward which the society should strive. Any number of practical reasons may prevent the society from moving rapidly toward this ideal. But this does not mean that the statement of and devotion to the ideal are without value. On the contrary, the educational policy of a country will depend on the clarity and enthusiasm with which its educational ideal is stated and believed.

The poverty of a country may seem to prevent it from rapid approximation of its educational ideal. In the past the education of the few rested on the labor of the many. It was assumed, perhaps rightly, that the few could not have education unless the many were deprived of it. Thomas Jefferson's proposal of three years of education for all could have been, and probably was, opposed on the ground that the economy of Virginia could not survive it. Whatever may have been the case in that state 150 years ago, and whatever may be the case today in underdeveloped countries, it can no longer be claimed that liberal education for all, from childhood to the grave, is beyond the economic powers of the United States.

The economic question can arise in another way. It can be suggested that liberal education is no good to a man who is starving, that the first duty of man is to earn a living, and that learning to earn a living and then earning it will absorb the time that might be devoted to liberal education in youth and maturity.

This argument is persuasive in countries where people are actually starving and where the economic system is at so rudimentary a stage that all a man's waking hours must be dedicated to extracting a meager livelihood from the soil. Undoubtedly the first task of the statesman in such countries is to raise the standard of living to such a point that the people may be freed from economic slavery and given the time to get the education appropriate to free men. Millions of men throughout the world are living in economic slavery. They are condemned to subhuman lives. We should do everything we can to strike the shackles from them. Even while we are doing so, we must remember that economic independence is not an end in itself; it is only a means, though an absolutely necessary one, to leading a human life. Even here, the clarity of the educational ideal that the society holds before itself, and the tenacity with which that ideal is pursued, are likely to be decisive of the fate of the society.

I have no doubt that a hundred years ago we thought of dear, little, far-off, feudal Japan in the same way in which we think of the underdeveloped countries today. With our assistance Japan became a full-fledged, industrialized world power in the space of forty years. We and the Japanese thought, in the 1860's, how wonderful it would be if this result could be achieved. We and they fixed our minds on the economic development of Japan and modified the educational system of that country on "American lines" to promote this economic development. So the rich got richer, the poor got poorer, the powerful got more bellicose; and Japan became a menace to the world and to itself.

No one can question the desirability of technical training in underdeveloped countries. No one can be satisfied with technical training as an ideal. The ideal is liberal education, and technical training can be justified only because it may help to supply the economic base that will make universal liberal education possible.

In developed countries technical training is also necessary, just as work is necessary in such countries. But the West has already achieved such a standard of living that it cannot use economic backwardness as an excuse for failing to face the task of making liberal education available to all. As far as the United States is concerned, the reorganization of the educational system would make it possible for the system to make its contribution to the liberal education of the young by the time they reached the age of eighteen.

Think of the time that could be saved by the simple process of squeezing the waste, water, and frivolity out of American education. The American scheme of an eight-year elementary school, a four-year high school, and a four-year college, with graduate and professional work on top of that, is unique in the world, and we cannot congratulate ourselves on its uniqueness. No other country could afford the duplication that occurs in passing from one unit in the American system to another, or the inordinate length of time that is consumed by each unit. The tremendous waste of time in the American educational system must result in part from the fact that there is so much time to waste. A six-year elementary school, a three- or four-year high school, and a three- or four-year college would eliminate from two to four years of lost motion and leave plenty of time for liberal education.

The degree of leisure now enjoyed by the whole American people is such as to open liberal education to all adults if they knew where to find it. The industrial worker now has twenty hours of free time a week that his grandfather did not have. Neither in youth nor in his adult life does he need much training in order to learn how to make a living. The constant drive to simplify industrial operations will eventually mean —and means in many industries today—that only a few hours will be required to give the worker all the training he can use.

If we assume that the object of concentration on vocational training in the schools is what John Dewey's mistaken followers think it is, to help young people to achieve economic independence, then we must admit that under present conditions in the United States the effort is disproportionate to the results. And the effort to do something that is not worth doing drives out of education the kind of activity that should characterize it. This effort diverts our attention from the enormously difficult task of discovering what education should be and then introducing it into the schools.

Even before mechanization had gone as far as it has now, one factor prevented vocational training, or any other form of *ad hoc* instruction, from accomplishing what was expected of it, and that factor was the mobility of the American population. This was a mobility of every kind—in space, in occupation, and in economic position. Training given in one place for work in that place was thrown away because the persons trained were almost certain to live and work in another place, or in several other places. Training given in one kind of work was equally useless because the persons trained usually did several other kinds of work rather than the kind they were trained to do. The failure of *ad hoc* instruction is so obvious that it has contributed to the notion that education, or schooling, is really irrelevant to any important activities of life and is merely a period through which the young must pass because we do not know what else to do with them. Actually the failure of *ad hoc* instruction shows nothing but the failure of *ad hoc* instruction. It does not show that education is unimportant or that in a mobile, industrial society there is no education that can meet the needs of the people.

If we are to take the assembly line as the characteristic feature of Western industry, we must regard industrialization as at best a mixed blessing. The monotony, impersonality, and uncreativeness of such work supply strong justification for the movement toward a steady reduction in the hours of labor. But what if the time that is gained for life off the assembly line is wasted, as much of it is today, in pursuits that can only be described as subhuman? What if the man as he works on the line has nothing in his head?

As the business of earning a living has become easier and simpler, it has also become less interesting and significant; and all personal problems have become more perplexing. This fact, plus the fact of the disappearance of any education adequate to deal with it, has led to the development of all kinds of cults, through which the baffled worker seeks some meaning for his life, and to the extension on an unprecedented scale of the most trivial recreations, through which he may hope to forget that his human problems are unsolved.

Adam Smith stated the case long ago: "A man without the proper use of the intellectual faculties of a man, is, if possible, more contemptible than even a coward, and seems to be mutilated and deformed in a still more essential part of the character of human nature." He points out that this is the condition of "the great body of the people," who, by the division of labor are confined in their employment "to a few very simple operations" in which the worker "has no occasion to exert his understanding, or to exercise his invention in finding out expedients for removing difficulties which never occur." The result, according to Smith, is that "the torpor of his mind renders him, not only incapable of relishing or bearing a part in any rational conversation, but of conceiving any generous, noble, or tender sentiment, and consequently of forming any just judgment concerning many even of the ordinary duties of private life."

Yet the substitution of machines for slaves gives us an opportunity to build a civilization as glorious as that of the Greeks, and far more lasting because far more just. I do not concede that torpor of mind is the natural and normal condition of the mass of mankind, or that these people are necessarily incapable of relishing or bearing a part in any rational conversation, or of conceiving generous, noble, and tender sentiments, or of forming just judgments concerning the affairs of private and public life. If they are so, and if they are so as a result of the division of labor, then industrialization and democracy are fundamentally opposed; for people in this condition are not qualified to govern themselves. I do not believe that industrialization and democracy are inherently opposed. But they are in actual practice opposed unless the gap between them is bridged by liberal education for all. That mechanization which tends to reduce a man to a robot also supplies the economic base and the leisure that will enable him to get a liberal education and to become truly a man.

CHAPTER IV

The Disappearance of Liberal Education

⚜ THE countries of the West are committed to universal, free, compulsory education. The United States first made this commitment and has extended it further than any other. In this country 92.5% of the children who are fourteen years old and 71.3% of those between fourteen and seventeen are in school. It will not be suggested that they are receiving the education that the democratic ideal requires. The West has not accepted the proposition that the democratic ideal demands liberal education for all. In the United States, at least, the prevailing opinion seems to be that the demands of that ideal are met by universal schooling, rather than by universal liberal education. What goes on in school is regarded as of relatively minor importance. The object appears to be to keep the child off the labor market and to detain him in comparatively sanitary surroundings until we are ready to have him go to work.

THE DISAPPEARANCE OF LIBERAL EDUCATION

The results of universal, free, compulsory education in America can be acceptable only on the theory that the object of the schools is something other than education, that it is, for example, to keep the young from cluttering up homes and factories during a difficult period of their lives, or that it is to bring them together for social or recreational purposes.

These last purposes, those which are social and recreational, the American educational system, on a very low level, achieves. It throws young people together. Since this does not take any greater effort than is required to pass compulsory school laws and build buildings, the accomplishment of this purpose would not at first blush seem to be a matter for boasting. Yet we often hear of it as something we should be proud of, and even as something that should suggest to us the main line of a sound educational policy. We often hear that bringing young people together, having them work and play together, and having them organize themselves "democratically" are the great contributions to democracy that the educational system can make. This is an expansion of the doctrine that was popular in my youth about the moral benefits conferred on everybody through intercollegiate athletics, which was, in turn, an adaptation of the remark dubiously imputed to the Duke of Wellington about the relationship between the battle of Waterloo and the playing fields of Eton.

No one can deny the value of getting together, of learning to get along with others, of coming to appreciate the methods of organization and the duties of membership in an organization any more than one can deny the importance of physical health and sportsmanship. It seems on the face of it a trifle absurd, however, to go to the trouble of training and engaging teachers, of erecting laboratories and libraries, and of laying out a program of instruction and learning if, in effect, the curriculum is extra and the extra-curriculum is the heart of the matter.

25

THE GREAT CONVERSATION

It seems doubtful whether the purposes of the educational system can be found in the pursuit of objects that the Boy Scouts, the Y.M.C.A., and the local country club, to say nothing of the family and the church, purport to be pursuing. The unique function of the educational system would appear to have something to do with the mind. No other agency in the community sets itself up, or is set up, to train the mind. To the extent to which the educational system is diverted to other objects, to that extent the mind of the community is neglected.

This is not to say that the educational system should not contribute to the physical, social, and moral development of those committed to its charge. But the method of its contribution, apart from the facilities for extra-curriculum activities that it provides, is through the mind. The educational system seeks to establish the rational foundations for good physical, moral, and social behavior. These rational foundations are the result of liberal education.

Education is supposed to have something to do with intelligence. It was because of this connection that it was always assumed that if the people were to have political power they would have to have education. They would have to have it if they were to use their power intelligently. This was the basis of the Western commitment to universal, free, compulsory education. I have suggested that the kind of education that will develop the requisite intelligence for democratic citizenship is liberal education, education through great books and the liberal arts, a kind of education that has all but disappeared from the schools, colleges, and universities of the United States.

Why did this education disappear? It was the education of the Founding Fathers. It held sway until fifty years ago. Now it is almost gone. I attribute this phenomenon to two factors, internal decay and external confusion.

26

THE DISAPPEARANCE OF LIBERAL EDUCATION

By the end of the first quarter of this century great books and the liberal arts had been destroyed by their teachers. The books had become the private domain of scholars. The word "classics" came to be limited to those works which were written in Greek and Latin. Whitehead refers to Wordsworth's remark about men of science who "murder to dissect" and properly observes: "In the past, classical scholars have been veritable assassins compared to them." The classical books, it was thought, could be studied only in the original languages, and a student might attend courses in Plato and Lucretius for years without discovering that they had any ideas. His professors were unlikely to be interested in ideas. They were interested in philological details. The liberal arts in their hands degenerated into meaningless drill.

Their reply to criticism and revolt was to demand, forgetting that interest is essential in education, that their courses be required. By the end of the first quarter of this century the great Greek and Latin writers were studied only to meet requirements for entrance to or graduation from college. Behind these tariff walls the professors who had many of the great writers and much of the liberal arts in their charge contentedly sat, oblivious of the fact that they were depriving the rising generation of an important part of their cultural heritage and the training needed to understand it, and oblivious also of the fact that they were depriving themselves of the reason for their existence.

Philosophy, history, and literature, and the disciplines that broke away from philosophy—political science, sociology, and psychology—suffered from another kind of decay, which resulted from a confusion that I shall refer to later, a confusion about the nature and scope of the scientific method. This confusion widened the break between those disciplines that split off from philosophy; it led professors of these disciplines up many blind alleys; and it produced profound changes in philosophical study. The same influences cut the heart out of the study of history and literature.

In general the professors of the humanities and the social sciences and history, fascinated by the marvels of experimental natural science, were overpowered by the idea that similar marvels could be produced in their own fields by the use of the same methods. They also seemed convinced that any results obtained in these fields by any other methods were not worth achieving. This automatically ruled out writers previously thought great who had had the misfortune to live before the method of empirical natural science had reached its present predominance and who had never thought of applying it to problems and subject matters outside the range of empirical natural science. The insights of these writers were at once out of date; for they could, in the nature of the case, represent little but prejudice or guesswork, which it would be the object of the scientific method to sweep out of the way of progress.

Since the aim of philosophers, historians, and critics of literature and art, to say nothing of social scientists, was to be as "scientific" as possible, they could not concern themselves much with ideas or with the "unscientific" tradition of the West. Nor could they admit the utility of the liberal arts, apart from those associated with mathematics.

Meanwhile the idea of education for all became firmly established in the United States. The school-leaving age steadily rose. An unprecedented flood of pupils and students overwhelmed the schools, colleges, and universities, a flood that has gone on growing, with minor fluctuations, to this day. Merely to house and staff the educational enterprise was an undertaking that would have put a strain on the wealth and intelligence of any country.

The triumphs of industrialization, which made this educational expansion possible, resulted from triumphs of technology, which rested on triumphs of science, which were promoted by specialization. Specialization, experimental science, technology, and industrialization were new. Great books and the liberal arts were identified in the public mind with dead languages, arid routines, and an archaic, pre-scientific past. The march of progress could be speeded by getting rid of them, the public thought, and using scientific method and specialization for the double purpose of promoting technological advance and curing the social maladjustments that industrialization brought with it. This program would have the incidental value of restoring interest to its place in education and of preparing the young to take part in the new, specialized, scientific, technological, industrial, democratic society that was emerging, to join in raising the standard of living and in solving the dreadful problems that the effort to raise it was creating.

The revolt against the classical dissectors and drillmasters was justified. So was the new interest in experimental science. The revolt against liberal education was not justified. Neither was the belief that the method of experimental science could replace the methods of history, philosophy, and the arts. As is common in educational discussion, the public had confused names and things. The dissectors and drillmasters had no more to do with liberal education than the ordinary college of liberal arts has to do with those arts today. And the fact that a method obtains sensational results in one field is no guarantee that it will obtain any results whatever in another.

Do science, technology, industrialization, and specialization render the Great Conversation irrelevant?

We have seen that industrialization makes liberal education more necessary than ever, and that the leisure it provides makes liberal education possible, for the first time, for everybody.

29

THE GREAT CONVERSATION

We have observed that the reorganization of the educational system would enable everybody to get a liberal education and to become a specialist as well.

I should like to add that specialization, instead of making the Great Conversation irrelevant, makes it more pertinent than ever. Specialization makes it harder to carry on any kind of conversation; but this calls for greater effort, not the abandonment of the attempt.

There can be little argument about the proposition that the task of the future is the creation of a community. Community seems to depend on communication. This requirement is not met by improvements in transportation or in mail, telegraph, telephone, or radio services. These technological advances are frightening, rather than reassuring, and disruptive, rather than unifying, in such a world as we have today. They are the means of bringing an enemy's bombs or propaganda into our homes.

The effectiveness of modern methods of communication in promoting a community depends on whether there is something intelligible and human to communicate. This, in turn, depends on a common language, a common stock of ideas, and common human standards. These the Great Conversation affords. Reading these books should make a man feel himself a member of the species and tradition that these books come from. He should recognize the ties that bind him to his fellow members of the species and tradition. He should be able to communicate, in a real sense, with other men.

Must the specialist be excluded from the community? If so, there can hardly be one; for increasingly in the West everybody is a specialist. The task is to have a community nevertheless, and to discover means of using specialties to promote it. This can be done through the Great Conversation. Through it the expert can discover the great common principles that underlie the specialties. Through it he can bring ideas to bear upon his experience. In the light of the Great Conversation his special brand of knowledge loses its particularistic vices and becomes a means of penetrating the great books. The mathematical specialist, for example, can get further faster into the great mathematicians than a reader who is without his specialized training. With the help of great books, specialized knowledge can radiate out into a genuine interfiltration of common learning and common life.

Imagine the younger generation studying great books and learning the liberal arts. Imagine an adult population continuing to turn to the same sources of strength, inspiration, and communication. We could talk to one another then. We should be even better specialists than we are today because we could understand the history of our specialty and its relation to all the others. We would be better citizens and better men. We might turn out to be the nucleus of the world community.

CHAPTER V

Experimental Science

℀ THE Great Conversation began before the beginnings of experimental science. But the birth of the Conversation and the birth of science were simultaneous. The earliest of the pre-Socratics were investigating and seeking to understand natural phenomena; among them were men who used mathematical notions for this purpose. Even experimentation is not new; it has been going on for hundreds of years. But faith in the experiment as an exclusive method is a modern manifestation. The experimental method has won such clear and convincing victories that it is now regarded in some quarters not only as the sole method of building up scientific knowledge, but also as the sole method of obtaining knowledge of any kind.

Thus we are often told that any question that is not answerable by the empirical methods of science is not really answerable at all, or at least not by significant and verifiable statements. Exceptions may be made with regard to the kinds of questions mathematicians or logicians answer by their methods. But all other questions must be submitted to the methods of experimental research or empirical inquiry.

If they are not answerable by these methods, they are the sort of questions that should never have been asked in the first place. At best they are questions we can answer only by guesswork or conjecture; at worst they are meaningless or, as the saying goes, nonsensical questions. Genuinely significant problems, in contrast, get their meaning in large part from the scientific operations of observation, experiment, and measurement by which they can be solved; and the solutions, when discovered by these methods, are better than guesswork or opinion. They are supported by fact. They have been tested and are subject to further verification.

We are told furthermore that the best answers we can obtain by the scientific method are never more than probable. We must free ourselves, therefore, from the illusion that, outside of mathematics and logic, we can attain necessary and certain truth. Statements that are not mathematical or logical formulae may look as if they were necessarily or certainly true, but they only look like that. They cannot really be either necessary or certain. In addition, if they have not been subjected to empirical verification, they are, far from being necessarily true, not even established as probable. Such statements can be accepted provisionally, as working assumptions or hypotheses, if they are acceptable at all. Perhaps it is better, unless circumstances compel us to take another course, not to accept such statements at all.

Consider, for example, statements about God's existence or the immortality of the soul. These are answers to questions that cannot be answered—one way or the other—by the experimental method. If that is the only method by which probable and verifiable knowledge is attainable, we are debarred from having knowledge about God's existence or the immortality of the soul. If modern man, accepting the view that he can claim to know only what can be demonstrated by experiment or verified by empirical research, still wishes to believe in these things, he must acknowledge that he does so by religious faith or by the exercise of his will to believe; and he must be prepared to be regarded in certain quarters as hopelessly superstitious.

It is sometimes admitted that many propositions that are affirmed by intelligent people, such as that democracy is the best form of government or that world peace depends upon world government, cannot be tested by the method of experimental science. But it is suggested that this is simply because the method is still not fully developed. When our use of the method matures, we shall find out how to employ it in answering every genuine question.

Since many propositions in the Great Conversation have not been arrived at by experiment or have not been submitted to empirical verification, we often hear that the Conversation, though perhaps interesting to the antiquarian as setting forth the bizarre superstitions entertained by "thinkers" before the dawn of experimental science, can have no relevance for us now, when experimental science and its methods have at last revealed these superstitions for what they are. We are urged to abandon the reactionary notion that the earlier voices in the Conversation are even now saying something worth listening to, and supplicated to place our trust in the experimental method as the only source of valid or verifiable answers to questions of every sort.

One voice in the Great Conversation itself announces this modern point of view. In the closing paragraph of his *Enquiry Concerning Human Understanding*, David Hume writes: "When we run over libraries, persuaded of these principles, what havoc must we make? If we take in our hand any volume

34

. . . let us ask, *Does it contain any abstract reasoning concerning quantity or number?* No. *Does it contain any experimental reasoning concerning matter of fact and existence?* No. Commit it then to the flames: for it can contain nothing but sophistry and illusion."

The books that Hume and his followers, the positivists of our own day, would commit to burning or, what is the same, to dismissal from serious consideration, do not reflect ignorance or neglect of Hume's principles. Those books, written after as well as before Hume, argue the case against the kind of positivism that asserts that everything except mathematics and experimental science is sophistry and illusion. They state and defend propositions quite opposite to those of Hume.

The Great Conversation, in short, contains both sides of the issue that in modern times is thought to have a most critical bearing on the significance of the Great Conversation itself. Only an unashamed dogmatist would dare to assert that the issue has been finally resolved now in favor of the view that, outside of logic or mathematics, the method of modern science is the *only* method to employ in seeking knowledge. The dogmatist who made this assertion would have to be more than unashamed. He would have to blind himself to the fact that his own assertion was not established by the experimental method, nor made as an indisputable conclusion of mathematical reasoning or of purely logical analysis.

With regard to this issue about the scientific method, which has become central in our own day, the contrary claim is not made for the Great Conversation. It would be equally dogmatic to assert that the issue has been resolved in favor of the opposite point of view. What can be justly claimed, however, is that the great books ably present both sides of the issue and throw light on aspects of it that are darkly as well as dogmatically treated in contemporary discussion.

They raise the question for us of what is meant by science

35

and the scientific method. If all that is meant is that a scientist is honest and careful and precise, and that he weighs all the evidence with discrimination before he pronounces judgment, then we can agree that the scientific method is the only method of reaching and testing the truth in any field. But this conception of the scientific method is so broad as to include the methods used by competent historians, philosophers, and theologians since the beginning of time; and it is not helpful, indeed it is seriously misleading, to name a method used in all fields after one of them.

Sometimes the scientific method seems to mean that we must pay attention to the facts, which carries with it the suggestion that those who do not believe that the method of experimental science is appropriate to every other field of inquiry do not pay attention to the facts and are therefore remote from reality. The great books show, on the contrary, that even those thinkers of the past who are now often looked upon as the most reactionary, the medieval theologians, insisted, as Aristotle had before them, that the truth of any statement is its conformity to reality or fact, and that sense-experience is required to discover the particular matters of fact that test the truth of general statements about the nature of things.

"In the knowledge of nature," Aristotle writes, the test of principles "is the unimpeachable evidence of the senses as to each fact." He holds that "lack of experience diminishes our power of taking a comprehensive view of the admitted facts. Hence those who dwell in intimate association with nature and its phenomena grow more and more able to formulate, as the foundation of their theories, principles such as to admit of a wide and coherent development; while those whom devotion to abstract discussions has rendered unobservant of the facts are too ready to dogmatize on the basis of a few observations." Theories should be credited, Aristotle insists,

"only if what they affirm agrees with the observed facts."
Centuries later, an experimental physiologist such as William
Harvey says neither more nor less when he declares that "to
test whether anything has been well or ill advanced, to as-
certain whether some falsehood does not lurk under a proposition, it is imperative on us to bring it to the proof of sense,
and to admit or reject it on the decision of sense."

To proclaim the necessity of observing the facts, and all the
facts, is not to say, however, that merely collecting facts will
solve a problem of any kind. The facts are indispensable; they
are not sufficient. To solve a problem it is necessary to think.
It is necessary to think even to decide what facts to collect.
Even the experimental scientist cannot avoid being a liberal
artist, and the best of them, as the great books show, are men
of imagination and of theory as well as patient observers of
particular facts. Those who have condemned thinkers who
have insisted on the importance of ideas have often over-
looked the equal insistence of these writers on obtaining the
facts. These critics have themselves frequently misunderstood
the scientific method and have confused it with the aimless
accumulation of data.

When the various meanings of science and the scientific
method are distinguished and clarified, the issue remains
whether the method associated with experimental science,
as that has developed in modern times, is the only method of
seeking the truth about what really exists or about what men
and societies should do. As already pointed out, both sides
of this issue are taken and argued in the Great Conversation.
But the great books do more than that. They afford us the
best examples of man's efforts to seek the truth, both about
the nature of things and about human conduct, by methods
other than those of experimental science; and because these
examples are presented in the context of equally striking
examples of man's efforts to learn by experiment or the

method of empirical science, the great books provide us with the best materials for judging whether the experimental method is or is not the only acceptable method of inquiry into all things.

That judgment the reader of the great books must finally make for himself. When he makes it in the light of the best examples of the employment of different methods to solve the problems of different subject matters, he will not have begged the question, as do those who, before reading the great books, judge them in terms of the dogma that there is only one method and that, though there are obvious differences among subject matters, no knowledge about any subject matter can be achieved unless this one method is applied.

On one point there seems to be no question. The contemporary practices of scientific research, as well as the scientific efforts that the great books record, show beyond doubt that the method of the controlled experiment under artificial conditions is not the only method used by men who regard themselves and are regarded as scientists. It may represent the most perfect form of empirical inquiry. It may be the model on which all the less exact forms of scientific investigation are patterned. But as the work of astronomers, biologists, and social scientists reveals, experiment in the strict sense is not always possible.

The method of the controlled experiment under artificial conditions is exclusively the method of that part of science the subject matter of which permits it to be experimental. On the assumption that nonliving matter always behaves in the same way under the same conditions, we are justified in concluding from experiment that we have discovered how certain nonliving matter behaves under certain conditions. On the assumption that living matter, when very large numbers of units are taken into account, is likely to exhibit uniformities of behavior under identical conditions, we are justified in concluding that if we know the conditions are identical, which is possible only in the laboratory, and if we know that the number of units under examination is large enough, then probably such uniformities of behavior as we detect will recur under identical conditions.

The griefs and losses sustained by those social scientists who predict the outcome of horse races and presidential elections are sufficient to indicate the difficulties of their subject. No one would propose that the social scientists should not keep on trying. The more refined and complete our knowledge of society, the better off we shall be. But it would be helpful to the social scientists if they recognized that in understanding human beings, who often cannot be subjected to experiment in the laboratory like guinea pigs and atoms, the method of experimental science cannot, in the nature of things, produce results that can compare with those which science achieves in dealing with matters more susceptible to experimentation.

One eminent social scientist, Professor Robert Redfield, has suggested that his colleagues consider their relation to the humanities as well as to the natural sciences. "The imitation of the physical and biological sciences," he says, "has proceeded to a point where the fullest development of social science is hampered." Identification with the natural sciences shelters the social scientist "from a stimulation from philosophy and the arts and literature which social science needs . . . The stimulation which the social scientists can gain from the humanities can come from the arts and literature themselves, and through an understanding of some of the problems which interest philosophers and the more imaginative students of the creative productions of mankind."

According to Professor Redfield, the bond that links the social scientist and the humanist is their common subject matter. "Humanity," he says, "is the common subject-matter of those who look at men as they are represented in books or works of art, and of those who look at men as they appear in institutions and in directly visible action. It is the central and essential matter of interest to social scientist and humanist alike." Though they differ in their methods, they "share a common effort, a common interest"; and Redfield adds, "it may be doubted if the results so far achieved by the social scientists are more communicative of the truth about human nature than are the results achieved by the more personal and imaginative methods of the artist."

We should remember such sound advice when we are urged to abandon methods that have yielded important insights in favor of one that will doubtless be helpful, but may not be able to tell us everything we need to know. It may be unwise to reject the sources of wisdom that have been traditionally found in history, philosophy, and the arts. These disciplines do not give us mathematical knowledge or knowledge acquired in the laboratory, but to say that for these reasons what they give us is not knowledge in any sense is to disregard the facts and to put the world of knowable things in a dogmatic strait jacket.

The rise of experimental science has not made the Great Conversation irrelevant. Experimental science is a part of the Conversation. As Étienne Gilson has remarked, "our science is a part of our humanism" as "the science of Pericles' time was a part of Greek humanism." Science is itself part of the Great Conversation. In the Conversation we find science raising issues about knowledge and reality. In the light of the Conversation we can reach a judgment about the question in dispute: How many valid methods of inquiry are there?

Because of experimental science we now know a very large number of things about the natural world of which our predecessors were ignorant. In this set of books we can observe the birth of science, applaud the development of the experimental technique, and celebrate the triumphs it has won. But we can also note the limitations of the method and mourn the errors that its misapplication has caused. We can distinguish the outlines of those great persistent problems that the method of experimental natural science may never solve and find the clues to their solutions offered by other disciplines and other methods.

Education for All

X WE have seen that education through the liberal arts and great books is the best education for the best. We have seen that the democratic ideal requires the attempt to help everybody get this education. We have seen that none of the great changes, the rise of experimental science, specialization, and industrialization, makes this attempt irrelevant. On the contrary, these changes make the effort to give everybody this education more necessary and urgent.

We must now return to the most important question, which is: Can everybody get this education? When an educational ideal is proposed, we are entitled to ask in what measure it can be achieved. If it cannot be achieved at all, those who propose it may properly be accused of irresponsibility or disingenuousness.

Such accusations have in fact been leveled against those

42

who propose the ideal of liberal education for all. Many sincere democrats believe that those who propose this ideal must be antidemocratic. Some of these critics are carried away by an educational version of the doctrine of guilt by association. They say, "The ideal that you propose was put forward by and for aristocrats. Aristocrats are not democrats. Therefore neither you nor your ideal is democratic."

The answer to this criticism has already been given. Liberal education was aristocratic in the sense that it was the education of those who enjoyed leisure and political power. If it was the right education for those who had leisure and political power, then it is the right education for everybody today.

That all should be well acquainted with and each in his measure actively and continuously engaged in the Great Conversation that man has had about what is and should be does not seem on the face of it an antidemocratic desire. It is only antidemocratic if, in the name of democracy, it is erecting an ideal for all that all cannot in fact achieve. But if this educational ideal is actually implicit in the democratic ideal, as it seems to be, then it should not be refused because of its association with a past in which the democratic ideal was not accepted.

Many convinced believers in liberal education attack the ideal of liberal education for all on the ground that if we attempt to give liberal education to everybody we shall fail to give it to anybody. They point to the example of the United States, where liberal education has virtually disappeared, and say that this catastrophe is the inevitable result of taking the dogma of equality of educational opportunity seriously.

The two criticisms I have mentioned come to the same thing: that liberal education is too good for the people. The first group of critics and the second unite in saying that only the few can acquire an education that was the best for the

43

best. The difference between the two is in the estimate they place on the importance of the loss of liberal education.

The first group says that, since everybody cannot acquire a liberal education, democracy cannot require that anybody should have it. The second group says that, since everybody cannot acquire a liberal education, the attempt to give it to everybody will necessarily result in an inferior education for everybody. The remedy is to segregate the few who are capable from the many who are incapable and see to it that the few, at least, receive a liberal education. The rest can be relegated to vocational training or any kind of activity in school that happens to interest them.

The more logical and determined members of this second group of critics will confess that they believe that the great mass of mankind is and of right ought to be condemned to a modern version of natural slavery. Hence there is no use wasting educational effort upon them. They should be given such training as will be necessary to enable them to survive. Since all attempts to do more will be frustrated by the facts of life, such attempts should not be made.

Because the great bulk of mankind have never had the chance to get a liberal education, it cannot be "proved" that they can get it. Neither can it be "proved" that they cannot. The statement of the ideal, however, is of value in indicating the direction that education should take. For example, if it is admitted that the few can profit by liberal education, then we ought to make sure that they, at least, have the chance to get it.

It is almost impossible for them to do so in the United States today. Many claims can be made for the American people; but nobody would think of claiming that they can read, write, and figure. Still less would it be maintained that they understand the tradition of the West, the tradition in which they live. The products of American high schools are

44

illiterate; and a degree from a famous college or university is no guarantee that the graduate is in any better case. One of the most remarkable features of American society is that the difference between the "uneducated" and the "educated" is so slight.

The reason for this phenomenon is, of course, that so little education takes place in American educational institutions. But we still have to wrestle with the question of why this should be so. Is there so little education in the American educational system because that system is democratic? Are democracy and education incompatible? Do we have to say that, if everybody is to go to school, the necessary consequence is that nobody will be educated?

Since we do not know that everybody cannot get a liberal education, it would seem that, if this is the ideal education, we ought to try to help everybody get it. Those especially who believe in "getting the facts" and "the experimental method" should be the first to insist that until we have tried we cannot be certain that we shall fail.

The business of saying, in advance of a serious effort, that the people are not capable of achieving a good education is too strongly reminiscent of the opposition to every extension of democracy. This opposition has always rested on the allegation that the people were incapable of exercising intelligently the power they demanded. Always the historic statement has been verified: you cannot expect the slave to show the virtues of the free man unless you first set him free. When the slave has been set free, he has, in the passage of time, become indistinguishable from those who have always been free.

There appears to be an innate human tendency to underrate the capacity of those who do not belong to "our" group. Those who do not share our background cannot have our ability. Foreigners, people who are in a different economic status, and the young seem invariably to be regarded as intellectually backward, and constitutionally so, by natives, people in "our" economic status, and adults.

In education, for example, whenever a proposal is made that looks toward increased intellectual effort on the part of students, professors will always say that the students cannot do the work. My observation leads me to think that what this usually means is that the professors cannot or will not do the work that the suggested change requires. When, in spite of the opposition of the professors, the change has been introduced, the students, in my experience, have always responded nobly.

We cannot argue that, because those Irish peasant boys who became priests in the Middle Ages or those sons of American planters and businessmen who became the Founding Fathers of our country were expected as a matter of course to acquire their education through the liberal arts and great books, every person can be expected as a matter of course to acquire such an education today. We do not know the intelligent quotients of the medieval priests or of the Founding Fathers; they were probably high.

But such evidence as we have in our own time, derived from the experience of two or three colleges that have made the Great Conversation the basis of their course of study and from the experience of that large number of groups of adults who for the past eight years have been discussing great books in every part of the United States, suggests that the difficulties of extending this educational program to everybody may have been exaggerated.

Great books are great teachers; they are showing us every day what ordinary people are capable of. These books came out of ignorant, inquiring humanity. They are usually the first announcements of success in learning. Most of them were written for, and addressed to, ordinary people.

If many great books seem unreadable and unintelligible to

46

the most learned as well as to the dullest, it may be because we have not for a long time learned to read by reading them. Great books teach people not only how to read them, but also how to read all other books.

This is not to say that any great book is altogether free from difficulty. As Aristotle remarked, learning is accompanied by pain. There is a sense in which every great book is always over the head of the reader; he can never fully comprehend it. That is why the books in this set are infinitely rereadable. That is why these books are great teachers; they demand the attention of the reader and keep his intelligence on the stretch.

As Whitehead has said, "Whenever a book is written of real educational worth, you may be quite certain that some reviewer will say that it will be difficult to teach from it. Of course it will be difficult to teach from it. If it were easy, the book ought to be burned; for it cannot be educational. In education, as elsewhere, the broad primrose path leads to a nasty place."

But are we to say that because these books are more difficult than detective stories, pulp magazines, and textbooks, therefore they are to remain the private property of scholars? Are we to hold that different rules obtain for books on the one hand and painting, sculpture, and music on the other? We do not confine people to looking at poor pictures and listening to poor music on the ground that they cannot understand good pictures and good music. We urge them to look at as many good pictures and hear as much good music as they can, convinced that this is the way in which they will come to understand and appreciate art and music. We would not recommend inferior substitutes, because we would be sure that they would degrade the public taste rather than lead it to better things.

If only the specialist is to be allowed access to these

47

books, on the ground that it is impossible to understand them without "scholarship," if the attempt to understand them without "scholarship" is to be condemned as irremediable superficiality, then we shall be compelled to shut out the majority of mankind from some of the finest creations of the human mind. This is aristocracy with a vengeance.

Sir Richard Livingstone said, "No doubt a trained student will understand Aeschylus, Plato, Erasmus, and Pascal better than the man in the street; but that does not mean that the ordinary man cannot get a lot out of them. Am I not allowed to read Dante because he is full of contemporary allusions and my knowledge of his period is almost nil? Or Shakespeare, because if I had to do a paper on him in the Oxford Honours School of English literature, I should be lucky to get a fourth class? Am I not to look at a picture by Velasquez or Cézanne, because I shall understand and appreciate them far less than a painter or art critic would? Are you going to postpone any acquaintance with these great things to a day when we are all sufficiently educated to understand them—a day that will never come? No, no. Sensible people read great books and look at great pictures knowing very little of Plato or Cézanne, or of the influences which moulded the thought or art of these men, quite aware of their own ignorance, but in spite of it getting a lot out of what they read or see."

Sir Richard goes on to refer to the remarks of T. S. Eliot: "In my own experience of the appreciation of poetry I have always found that the less I knew about the poet and his work, before I began to read it, the better. An elaborate preparation of historical and biographical knowledge has always been to me a barrier. It is better to be spurred to acquire scholarship because you enjoy the poetry, than to suppose that you enjoy the poetry because you have acquired the scholarship."

Even more important than the dogma of scholarship in keeping people from the books is the dogma of individual differences. This is one of the basic dogmas of American education. It runs like this: all men are different; therefore, all men require a different education; therefore, anybody who suggests that their education should be in any respect the same has ignored the fact that all men are different; therefore, nobody should suggest that everybody should read some of the same books; some people should read some books, some should read others. This dogma has gained such a hold on the minds of American educators that you will now often hear a college president boast that his college has no curriculum. Each student has a course of study framed, or "tailored" is the usual word, to meet his own individual needs and interests.

We should not linger long in discussing the question of whether a student at the age of eighteen should be permitted to determine the actual content of his education for himself. As we have a tendency to underrate the intelligence of the young, we have a tendency to overrate their experience and the significance of the expression of interests and needs on the part of those who are inexperienced. Educators ought to know better than their pupils what an education is. If educators do not, they have wasted their lives. The art of teaching consists in large part of interesting people in things that ought to interest them, but do not. The task of educators is to discover what an education is and then to invent the methods of interesting their students in it.

But I do not wish to beg the question. The question, in effect, is this: Is there any such thing as "an education"? The answer that is made by the devotees of the dogma of individual differences is No; there are as many different educations as there are different individuals; it is "authoritarian" to say that there is any education that is necessary, or even suitable, for every individual.

49

So Bertrand Russell once said to me that the pupil in school should study whatever he liked. I asked whether this was not a crime against the pupil. Suppose a boy did not like Shakespeare. Should he be allowed to grow up without knowing Shakespeare? And, if he did, would he not look back upon his teachers as cheats who had defrauded him of his cultural heritage? Lord Russell replied that he would require a boy to read one play of Shakespeare; if he did not like it, he should not be compelled to read any more.

I say that Shakespeare should be a part of the education of everybody. The point at which he is introduced into the course of study, the method of arousing interest in him, the manner in which he is related to the problems of the present may vary as you will. But Shakespeare should be there because of the loss of understanding, because of the impoverishment, that results from his absence. The comprehension of the tradition in which we live and our ability to communicate with others who live in the same tradition and to interpret our tradition to those who do not live in it are drastically affected by the omission of Shakespeare from the intellectual and artistic experience of any of us.

If any common program is impossible, if there is no such thing as an education that everybody ought to have, then we must admit that any community is impossible. All men are different; but they are also the same. As we must all become specialists, so we must all become men. In view of the ample provision that is now made for the training of specialists, in view of the divisive and disintegrative effects of specialism, and in view of the urgent need for unity and community, it does not seem an exaggeration to say that the present crisis calls first of all for an education that shall emphasize those respects in which men are the same, rather than those in which they are different. The West needs an education that draws out our common humanity rather than our individuality. Individual differences can be taken into account in the methods that are employed and in the opportunities for specialization that may come later.

In this connection we might recall the dictum of Rousseau: "It matters little to me whether my pupil is intended for the army, the church, or the law. Before his parents chose a calling for him, nature called him to be a man . . . When he leaves me, he will be neither a magistrate, a soldier, nor a priest; he will be a man."

If there is an education that everybody should have, how is it to be worked out? Educators are dodging their responsibility if they do not make the attempt; and I must confess that I regard the popularity of the dogma of individual differences as a manifestation of a desire on the part of educators to evade a painful but essential duty. The Editors of this set believe that these books should be central in education. But if anybody can suggest a program that will better accomplish the object they have in view, they will gladly embrace him and it.

❧ CHAPTER VII ❧

The Education of Adults

❧ THE Editors believe that these books should be read by all adults all their lives. They concede that this idea has novel aspects. The education of adults has uniformly been designed either to make up for the deficiencies of their schooling, in which case it might terminate when these gaps had been filled, or it has consisted of vocational training, in which case it might terminate when training adequate to the post in question had been gained.

What is here proposed is interminable liberal education. Even if the individual has had the best possible liberal education in youth, interminable education through great books and the liberal arts remains his obligation; he cannot expect to store up an education in childhood that will last all his life. What he can do in youth is to acquire the disciplines and habits that will make it possible for him to continue to educate himself all his life. One must agree with John Dewey in this: that continued growth is essential to intellectual life.

The twin aims that have animated mankind since the dawn of history are the conquest of nature and the conquest of drudgery. Now they seem in a fair way to be achieved. And the achievement seems destined, at the same time, to end in the trivialization of life. It is impossible to believe that men can long be satisfied with the kind of recreations that now occupy the bulk of their free time. After all, they are men. Man, though an animal, is not all animal. He is rational, and he cannot live by animal gratifications alone; still less by amusements that animals have too much sense to indulge in. A man must use his mind; he must feel that he is doing something that will develop his highest powers and contribute to the development of his fellow men, or he will cease to be a man.

The trials of the citizen now surpass anything that previous generations ever knew. Private and public propaganda beats upon him from morning till night all his life long. If independent judgment is the *sine qua non* of effective citizenship in a democracy, then it must be admitted that such judgment is harder to maintain now than it ever has been before. It is too much to hope that a strong dose of education in childhood and youth can inoculate a man to withstand the onslaughts on his independent judgment that society conducts, or allows to be conducted, against him every day. For this, constant mental alertness and mental growth are required.

The conception of liberal education for adults that is here advanced has an important effect on our conception of education in childhood and youth, its purpose and its content. If we are to expect the whole adult population to engage in liberal education, then the curriculum of schools, colleges, and universities should be constructed with this end in view. At present it is built upon the notion, which is unfortunately correct, that nobody is ever going to get any education after he gets out of school. Here we encounter the melancholy fact that most of the important things that human beings ought to understand cannot be comprehended in youth.

Although I have known several astronomers who were contributing to the international journals before the age of sixteen, I have never known a child of any age who had much that was useful to say about the organization of human society or the ends of human life. The great books of ethics, political philosophy, economics, history, and literature do not yield up their secrets to the immature. In the United States, if these works are read at all, they are read in school and college, where they can be only dimly understood, and are never read again. Hence Americans are unlikely to understand them fully; we are deprived of the light they might shed upon our present problems.

Here the theory that education must meet immediate needs comes in to complete the chaos in our educational institutions. If the aim of education is to meet the immediate needs of the person educated, and if he is never to have any more education after he gets out of educational institutions, then he must learn everything he might ever need while he is in these institutions. Since there is no way of telling what the graduate might need, the only way out is to offer him a little bit of everything, hoping that he will find some bits useful. So the American high school and college are jammed with miscellaneous information on every conceivable subject from acrobatics to zymurgy; for who can say that some future high-wire artist or brewer will not be found among the students? The great, wild proliferation of the curriculum of American schools, colleges, and universities is the result of many influences; but we can say with some assurance that if adult life had been looked upon as a time for continued learning, the pressure toward proliferation would have been measurably reduced.

A concern with liberal education for all adults is necessary if we are to have liberal education for anybody; because liberal education can flourish in the schools, colleges, and universities of a country only if the adult population understands and values it. The best way to understand and value something is to have it yourself.

We hear a great deal today about the neglect of the liberal arts colleges and the decay of humanistic and social studies. It is generally assumed that all that these colleges and scholars require is money. If they had more money, their problems would be solved. We are led to believe that their failure to get money results from the obtuseness or perversity of college and university presidents. These officers are supposed to be interested in the development of natural science and technology at the expense of the liberal arts and the humanistic and social studies.

One may be permitted to doubt whether the colleges of liberal arts and scholars in the humanities and the social studies could wisely spend more money than they have. The deficiencies of these institutions and individuals do not seem to result from lack of funds, but from lack of ideas. When the appeal for support of a college is based on the fact that its amenities are almost as gracious as those of the local country club; when scholars in the humanities and social studies, misled by their misconception of the scientific method and by the prestige of natural science, dedicate themselves to the aimless accumulation of data about trivial subjects, the problem does not seem to be financial. Unfortunately, the only problems that money can solve are financial problems.

Institutions and subjects develop because people think they are important. The importance comes first, and the money afterward. The importance of experimental science is obvious to everybody. Science produced the atomic bomb; and the medical schools are doing almost as much to lengthen life as the departments of physics and chemistry are doing to

55

shorten it. Many colleges of liberal arts and the researches of many scholars in the humanities and the social studies are important only to those whose livelihood depends upon them.

Yet the great issues are there. What is our destiny? What is a good life? How can we achieve a good society? What can we learn to guide us through the mazes of the future from history, philosophy, literature, and the fine arts?

These questions lie, for the most part, in the areas traditionally assigned to the liberal arts, the humanities, and the social studies. If through this set of books, or in any other way, the adult population of laymen came to regard these issues as important; if scholars in these fields were actually engaged in wrestling with these problems; if in a large number of homes all over the country these questions were being discussed, then two things would happen. It would become respectable for intelligent young people, young people with ideas, to devote their lives to the study of these issues, as it is respectable to be a scientist or an engineer today; and the colleges of liberal arts and scholars in the humanities and the social sciences would receive all the support they could use.

An axiomatic educational proposition is that what is honored in a country will be cultivated there. One object of this set of books is to do honor to the great tradition of the West, in the conviction that this is the way in which to promote its cultivation, elaboration, and extension, and to perpetuate it to posterity.

✗ CHAPTER VIII ✗

The Next Great Change

✗ SINCE education is concerned with the future, let us ask ourselves what we know positively about the future.

We know that all parts of the world are getting closer together in terms of the mechanical means of transportation and communication. We know that this will continue. The world is going to be unified, by conquest or consent.

We know that the fact that all parts of the world are getting closer together does not by itself mean greater unity or safety in the world. It may mean that we shall all go up in one great explosion.

We know that there is no defense against the most destructive of modern weapons. Both the victor and the defeated will lose the next war. All the factors that formerly protected this country, geographical isolation, industrial strength, and military power, are now obsolete.

We know that the anarchy of competing sovereign states must lead to war sooner or later. Therefore we must have world law, enforced by a world organization, which must be attained through world co-operation and community.

We know that it will be impossible to induce all men to agree on all matters. The most we can hope for is to induce all men to be willing to discuss all matters instead of shooting one another about some matters. A civilization in which all men are compelled to agree is not one in which we would care to live. Under such circumstances one world would be worse than many; for in many worlds there is at least the chance of escape from one to another. The only civilization in which a free man would be willing to live is one that conceives of history as one long conversation leading to clarification and understanding. Such a civilization presupposes communication; it does not require agreement.

We know that time is of the essence. Every day we read announcements of advances in transportation and "advances" in destruction. We can now go round the world in the time it used to take to go from New York to Boston; and we can kill a quarter of a million people with one bomb. We are promised bigger and better instruments of mass murder in every issue of our daily papers. At the same time the hostility among sovereign states is deepening by the hour.

How can we prepare for a future like this?

We see at once that the primary, not the incidental, participants in an educational program designed to cope with a future like this must be adults. They are in charge of the world. The rising generation, unless the adults in charge of the world can find some way of living together immediately, may never have a chance to rise.

I do not wish to exaggerate the possibilities of adult education through great books and the liberal arts, or by any other means, as a method of preventing war. If all the adults in America could suddenly realize their full human potentialities, which is the object of liberal education, and the government of Russia remained what it is today, we might merely have the satisfaction of being blown up with our full human potentialities realized instead of unrealized. In view of the prevailing skepticism about the immortality of the soul I cannot expect American readers to regard this as more than a dubious consolation.

Yet there will not be much argument against the proposition that, on the whole, reasonable and intelligent people, even if they confront aggressively unreasonable or stupid people, have a better chance of attaining their end, which in this case is peace, than if they are themselves unreasonable and stupid. They may even be able by their example to help their opponents to become more reasonable and less stupid.

The United States is now the most powerful country in the world. It has been a world power for a very short time. It has not had centuries of experience in which to learn how to discharge the responsibilities of a position into which it was catapulted against its will. Nor has it had the kind of education, in the last fifty years, that is conducive to understanding its position or to maintaining it with balance, dignity, and charity. An educational system that aims at vocational training, or social adjustment, or technological advance is not likely to lead to the kind of maturity that the present crisis demands of the most powerful nation in the world.

A country that is powerful, inexperienced, and uneducated can be a great danger to world peace. The United States is unlikely to endanger peace through malevolence. The people of this country do not appear to bear any ill-will toward any other people; nor do they want anything that any other people have. Since they are devoted to their own kind of society and government, they do not want any other nation to threaten the continued prosperity of their society and government. Any military moves made by the United States will be made in the conviction that they are necessary for the defense of this country.

But this conviction may be mistaken. It may be hysterical, or it may be ignorant. We can easily blunder into war. Since we may have committed such a blunder even before these words appear in print, I must repeat that I do not wish to exaggerate the importance of these books, or any other means of adult education, as a method of preventing such a blunder. The time is short, and education is long. What I am saying is that, since education is long, and since it is indispensable, we should begin it right away.

When Marshal Lyautey was in Africa, he asked his gardener to plant a certain tree, the foliage of which he liked very much. The gardener said that a tree of this kind took two hundred years to reach maturity. "In that case," said the marshal, "there is no time to lose. Plant it today."

The Great Conversation symbolizes that Civilization of the Dialogue which is the only civilization in which a free man would care to live. It promotes the realization of that civilization here and now. This set of books is organized on the principle of attaining clarification and understanding of the most important issues, as stated by the greatest writers of the West, through continuous discussion. Its object is to project the Great Conversation into the future and to have everybody participate in it. The community toward which it is hoped that these books may contribute is the community of free minds.

Now the only defense that any nation can have is the character and intelligence of its people. The adequacy of that defense will depend upon the strength of the conviction that the nation is worth defending. This conviction must rest on a comprehension of the values for which that nation stands. In the case of the United States those values are to be found in the tradition of the West. The tradition of the West is the Great Conversation.

We have repeated to ourselves so much of late the slogan, "America must be strong," that we have forgotten what strength is. We appear to believe that strength consists of masses of men and machines. I do not deny that they have their role. But surely the essential ingredients of strength are trained intelligence, love of country, the understanding of its ideals, and such devotion to those ideals that they become a part of the thought and life of every citizen.

We cannot hope to make ourselves intelligible to the rest of the world unless we understand ourselves. We now present a confusing picture to other peoples largely because we are ourselves confused. To take only one example, how can we say that we are a part of the great tradition of the West, the essence of which is that nothing is to be undiscussed, when some of our most representative citizens constantly demand the suppression of freedom of speech in the interest of national security? Now that military power is obsolescent, the national security depends on our understanding of and devotion to such ancient Western liberties as free speech. If we abandon our ideals under external pressure, we give away without a fight what we would be fighting for if we went to war. We abandon the sources of our strength.

How can we say that we are defending the tradition of the West if we do not know what it is? An educational program, for young people or adults, from which this tradition has disappeared, fails, of course, to transmit it to our own people. It also fails to convince other people that we are devoted to it as we claim. Any detached observer looking at the American educational system can see that the bulk of its activity is irrelevant to any of the things we know about the future.

Vocationalism, scientism, and specialism can at the most

assist our people to earn a living and thus maintain the economy of the United States. They cannot contribute to the much more important elements of national strength: trained intelligence, the understanding of the country's ideals, and devotion to them. Nor can they contribute to the growth of a community in this country. They are divisive rather than unifying forces. Vocational training, scientific experimentation, and specialization do not have to supplant liberal education in order to make their economic contribution. We can have liberal education for all and vocational training, scientific experimentation, and specialization, too.

We hear a great deal nowadays about international understanding, world community, and world organization. These things are all supposed to be good; but nothing very concrete is put forward as to the method by which they can be attained. We can be positive on one point: we are safe in saying that these things will not be brought about by vocational training, scientific experiment, and specialization. The kind of education we have for young people and adults in the United States today will not advance these causes. I should like to suggest one or two ways in which they may be advanced.

We should first dispose of the proposition that we cannot have world organization, a world of law, without a world community. This appears to overlook the obvious interaction between legal institutions and culture. As Aristotle pointed out long ago, law is itself an educational force. The Constitution of the United States educates the people every day to believe in and support the Constitution of the United States.

World community, in the sense of perfect understanding among all peoples everywhere, is not required in order to have the beginnings of world law. What is required is that minimum understanding which is sufficient to allow world law to begin. From that point forward world law will support world community and world community will support world law.

For example, there are those who oppose the discussion of universal disarmament on the ground that disarmament is an effect and not a cause. They say that, until the tensions in the world are removed, disarmament cannot take place and that we shall simply deceive ourselves if we talk about it instead of doing something about the tensions.

Actually one way to do something about the tensions is to talk about disarmament. The manifestation of a general willingness to disarm under effective international regulation and control would do more to relieve the tensions in the world than any other single thing. Getting together to see whether such a plan could be formulated would relieve tension. No doubt there would be disappointments, and the risk of exacerbating international irritations; but to refuse to discuss the principal method of mitigating tensions on the ground that they have to be mitigated before it is discussed does not seem to be the best way to mitigate them.

What are the best ways of promoting that minimum of understanding which is necessary to permit world law to begin? If community depends on communication, we must ask what kinds of things can be most readily communicated to and comprehended by the largest number of people, and what kinds of things tell the most about the people who are doing the communicating? It appears that the kind of things that are most intelligible and most revealing are ideas and artistic objects. They are most readily understood; they are most characteristic of the peoples who have produced or stated them.

We can learn more about another people from their artistic and intellectual productions than we can from all the statistics and data that can ever be collected. We can learn more, that is, of what we need to know in order to found a world community. We can learn more in the sense that we can understand more. What we have in this set of books is a means by which people who can read English can understand the West. We in the West can understand ourselves and one another; peoples in other parts of the world can understand us.

This leads to the idea that Scott Buchanan has put forward, the idea of a world republic of law and justice and a world republic of learning mutually supporting each other. Any republic maintains its justice, peace, freedom, and order by the exercise of intelligence. Every assent on the part of the governed is a product of learning. A republic is a common educational life in process. So Montesquieu said that as the principle of an aristocracy was honor, and the principle of a tyranny was fear, the principle of a democracy was education. Thomas Jefferson took him seriously. Now we discover that a little learning is a dangerous thing. We see now that we need more learning, more real learning, for everybody.

The republic of learning is that republic toward which all mere political republics gravitate, and which they must serve if they are to be true to themselves. No one saw this before yesterday, and we only today are able to begin to measure what we should do about it tomorrow. The immediate inference from this insight is a utopia for today, the extension of universal education to every man and woman, from childhood to the grave. It is time to take education away from the scholars and school teachers and to open the gates of the republic of learning to those who can and will make it responsible to humanity.

Learning is in principle and should be in fact the highest common good, to be defended as a right and worked for as an end. All men are capable of learning, according to their abilities. Learning does not stop as long as a man lives, unless his learning power atrophies because he does not use it. Political freedom cannot last without provision for the free unlimited acquisition of knowledge. Truth is not long retained in human affairs without continual learning and re-learning. A political order is tyrannical if it is not rational.

If we aim at a world republic of law and justice, we must recover and revive the great tradition of liberal human thought, rethink our knowledge in its light and shadow, and set up the devices of learning by which everybody can, perhaps for the first time, become a citizen of the world. The kind of understanding that comes through belonging to the world republic of learning is the kind that constitutes the world community. The world republic of law and justice is nothing but the political expression of the world republic of learning and the world community.

CHAPTER IX

East and West

❧ A̲T this point I hear some reader say, "The world community and the world republic of law and justice must be composed of all peoples everywhere. These are great books of the West. How can comprehension of the tradition they embody amount to participation in the world republic of learning? How can such comprehension promote world community, since great books of the East are not included?"

The Editors reply that there is undoubtedly to be a meeting of East and West. It is now going on, under rather unsatisfactory conditions. The Editors believe that those who come to the meeting with some grasp of the full range of the Western tradition will be more likely to understand the East than those who have attended any number of the hastily instituted survey courses about the East proposed by educators who have been suddenly impressed by the necessity of understanding the East and whose notion is that the way to understand anything is to get a lot of information about it.

The Editors are impressed by the many reminders given to the West by Eastern thinkers that the parts of the Western tradition that are now the least known and the least respected in America are the very parts most likely to help us understand the deepest thought of the East. On the other hand, the Editors are convinced that those aspects of the West which the East finds most terrifying, its materialism, rapacity, and ethnocentric pride, will get no support from those great books which indicate the main line of the Western pursuit of wisdom. The Editors believe that an education based on the full range of the Western search is far more likely to produce a genuine openness about the East, a genuine capacity to understand it, than any other form of education now proposed or practicable.

The West can try, as the saying goes, to "win" the East by coming to the meetings between them with a few words adjusted directly to the questions that arise from the manner in which the East is, as the saying goes, "awakening." There is no question that the West will inevitably be represented at these meetings by a good many of those social engineers who feel, in all ignorance, that they represent in splendor what twenty-five centuries of Western civilization have been laboring to produce. Scientific humanism, which has been vigorously and in high places presented as the new religion that the new one world needs, will certainly be represented. Some representatives will surely be making the offer of the magic trio: scientific method, technology, and the American Way of Life.

It seems safe to predict, however, that these representatives of the West are likely to be understood only by those in the East who have already decided for "westernization." These representatives of the West may be considerably nonplused by those in the East who are determined, however much they "awaken" in certain respects, to retain the central convictions and habits of thought of Eastern culture.

As Ananda Coomaraswamy has said, "It is true that there is a modernized, uprooted East, with which the West can *compete*; but it is only with the surviving, superstitious East —Gandhi's East, the one that has never attempted to live by bread alone—that the West can *co-operate*."

In seeking the co-operation of this modernized, uprooted East the Western social engineers will find themselves, as is already menacingly clear, competing with the rulers of the Soviet Union. These rulers are bringing to the meetings of East and West a far more ruthless version of this latter-day shrunken Western voice. Their words are adjusted far more directly to the exact questions that are involved in the "awakening" of the East. The Russians seem prepared to offer the new Easterners a program uncomplicated by any concern about the old East. Perhaps these new Easterners, under Russian guidance, may carry through a new kind of reflexive imperialism, more ruthless toward "the superstitious East, Gandhi's East," than any Western imperialist ever was.

If the East, contrary to its deepest traditions, becomes totally absorbed with material comfort, there will be little about the East that we shall have to understand, since we already understand that kind of absorption only too well. We have never pictured the East as coming to share it. If the East does come to share it, the change may shock us, but it will raise no very difficult question of understanding.

If, on the other hand, the awakening East tries to retain, beneath the new vigor of the drive toward material goods, its various forms of traditional religion, metaphysics, and ethics, the West, in trying to co-operate with the East, has something to understand.

Under these circumstances anyone anywhere, in or out of

68

the universities, who has attained some competence to bring forth a reading of the East that the West can understand, should be encouraged in every way to increase his competence and to make the results of his studies available. But the number of persons who can claim even such an initial competence is very small. Therefore it is absurd to suggest, as many laymen and scholars are doing today, that a large part of the course of study of our educational system should be devoted to "understanding the East."

Few persons are less helpful to the world than those educators, infatuated with the magic of curriculum changes, who think that the teachers or the teachability of any subject they dream of can spring into existence by curricular decree. It is irresponsible to suggest that the East can be given a major place in the education of everybody when no more than a handful of teachers exists who could decently commit themselves to the teaching of such courses. The "understanding" of the East that would emerge from such courses, taught by instructors who had hastily "read up" on the East, could set communication and understanding back for generations.

Professor John D. Wild of Harvard has lately commented on some educational proposals of Professor Howard Mumford Jones of Harvard. Mr. Wild says: "I gather that Mr. Jones is worried about our capacity really to understand Russia and to set up a co-operative world community. So am I. But I am unable to follow him in the assumption that these crucially important aims will be achieved merely by setting up more machinery, professors, and secretaries, more fields and areas called 'the study of Russia' and 'the study of the Orient'. *How* are these things to be studied; from what sort of integrating point of view? Is he proposing an amalgam of Western, Chinese, and Russian culture? If so, what would this be like? Or is he proposing a sort of cultural relativism in which every one seeks to divest himself so far as possible from all the culture he had? I do not believe that Mr. Jones is advocating either of these alternatives. I gather that he is interested in correcting the economic and social injustices that distort our present civilization, that he wishes to see the vast power which modern technology has put into our hands used intelligently for the common good. All this is in line with the best philosophical and religious thought of our western tradition, when properly understood. I gather further that he feels that we should be humble about the rather rudimentary civilization we now possess at this early stage, precious as it is, and that we should be open to suggestions from alien sources. This also is thoroughly in line with what is best in our own tradition. If this is what Mr. Jones means, then what we need most of all is to recall the basic insights and principles (religious as well as philosophical) upon which our western culture was founded, and then apply them to the critical problems of our time."

So also Professor Louis W. Norris: "Professor Jones has entered a strong and just plea for the relevance of education to its times. But there is grave danger here that the timeliness of education should obscure its timelessness. Socrates and Plato, as Professor Jones says, (and even more truly Aristotle) 'struggled with the local political problem.' But the very reason they were able to make such helpful comments about social, ethical and political questions was, that they were even more concerned to find out the 'forms' of things that were timeless. Without the 'definitions' of Socrates, the 'ideas' of Plato and the 'forms' of Aristotle, their 'radio commentating' would have been shallow gibberish, forgotten as soon as ninety-nine per cent of present commentary. A frantic concern to understand Russia or the Orient will lead us nowhere, unless the student brings to these problems skill in analysis, order in valuing, knowledge of history, and such social experience as gives him a basis for judging what he finds out about Russia and the Orient."

There is no reason why the West should feel that it must apologize for a determination to retain and renew a sense of its own character and its own range. Western civilization is one of the greatest civilizations to date. Not in a spirit of arrogance, but in a spirit of concern that nothing good be lost for the future, the West should take to its meetings with the East a full and vivid sense of its own achievements.

Nothing in the main line of the Western tradition leads to ethnocentric pride or cultural provincialism. If the West has been guilty of these sins, it is not because of its fidelity to its own character, but because of the many kinds of human weakness that always afflict any "successful" society.

Moreover, if we are to believe such an eminent student of this matter as Coomaraswamy, the Western tradition contains within itself elements that permit bridging to the deepest elements of Eastern traditions. Presumably we can build these bridges best if we understand the nature of the ground where the bridge begins.

Coomaraswamy says: "If ever the gulf between East and West, of which we are made continually more aware as physical intimacies are forced upon us, is to be bridged, it will be only by an agreement on principles. . . . A philosophy identical with Plato's is still a living force in the East. . . . Understanding requires a recognition of common values. For so long as men cannot think with other peoples, they have not understood, but only known them; and in this situation it is largely an ignorance of their own intellectual heritage that stands in the way of understanding and makes an unfamiliar way of thinking to seem 'queer'."

The irony here is that those who talk most about the need to change the course of study in order to promote understanding of the East would be those who would proclaim most loudly the obsolescence of those parts of the Western tradition (for example, Plato, Plotinus, Augustine, and the Western mystical and metaphysical tradition) which are perhaps equivalent, with some transformation, to the important parts of Eastern traditions. Such people would vigorously oppose an education requiring everybody to try to understand those things in the West which have the best chance of leading to a genuine understanding of the East; but for all that they vigorously propose that we understand the East.

The more dogmatic of those who feel that most of the Western tradition is obsolete, and who take scientific humanism as the new religion, are not likely to regard the problem of relations with the East as one of understanding, though they will use the phrase. They will see in the East little but backwardness, and will mark down Eastern ritual and mysticism as something scheduled for early technological demolition. One can imagine the indignant astonishment with which a beneficent American social engineer would greet the word of an earnest and respected student of the East, René Guénon, that "everything in the East is seen as the application and extension of a doctrine which in essence is purely intellectual and metaphysical."

Any widespread achievement of understanding between East and West will have to wait on the production of an adequate supply of liberally educated Westerners. Meanwhile, the problem is simply how to produce such a supply. The pretense that we are now prepared within the educational system at large to include understanding the East as one main pivot in a liberal curriculum will obstruct, not assist, the solution of the central problem of producing a liberally educated generation.

Unquestionably all the purposes that validate the publication of great books lead logically to Great Books of the

World, not of any part of the world. But at the moment we have all we can do to understand ourselves in order to be prepared for the forthcoming meetings between East and West. Those who want to add more great books of Eastern origin are deceiving themselves. The time for that will come when we have understood our own tradition well enough to understand another.

We may take to heart the message given the West by one of the great modern representatives of another culture. Charles Malik has said: "In all this we are really touching upon the great present crisis in western culture. We are saying when that culture mends its own spiritual fences, all will be well with the Near East, and not with the Near East alone. We are saying it is not a simple thing to be the heir of the Graeco-Roman-Christian-European synthesis and not to be true to its deepest visions. One can take the ten greatest spirits in that synthesis and have them judge the performance of the Western world in relation to the Near East. The deep problem of the Near East then must await the spiritual recovery of the West. And he does not know the truth who thinks that the West does not have in its own tradition the means and power wherewith it can once again be true to itself."

ℜ CHAPTER X ℤ

A Letter to the Reader

ℤ I IMAGINE you reading this far in this set of books for the purpose of discovering whether you should read further. I will assume that you have been persuaded of the necessity and possibility of reading these books in order to get a liberal education. But how about you? The Editors are not interested in general propositions about the desirability of reading the books; they want them read. They did not produce them as furniture for public or private libraries.

We say that these books contain a liberal education and that everybody ought to try to get one. You say either that you have had one, that you are not bright enough to get one, or that you do not need one.

You cannot have had one. If you are an American under the age of ninety, you can have acquired in the educational system only the faintest glimmerings of the beginnings of

74

liberal education. Ask yourself what whole great books you read while you were in school, college, or university. Ask yourself whether you and your teachers saw these books as a Great Conversation among the finest minds of Western history, and whether you obtained an understanding of the tradition in which you live. Ask yourself whether you mastered the liberal arts. I am willing to wager that, if you read any great books at all, you read very few, that you read one without reference to the others, in separate courses, and that for the most part you read only excerpts from them.

As for me, I was educated in two very "liberal" colleges. Apart from Shakespeare, who was scattered through my education, I read one of the books in this set, Goethe's *Faust*, and part of another, a few of the dialogues of Plato, as part of my formal education. I do not remember that I ever heard the name of Thomas Aquinas or Plotinus, when I was in college. I am not even sure that I heard of Karl Marx. I heard of many of the great scientific writers, but avoided association with them on the ground that they were too difficult for me—I gloried in the possession of an "unmathe-matical" mind—and I did not need to read them, because I was not going to be a scientist.

But suppose that you have in some way hammered out for yourself the kind of education that colleges ought to give. If you have done so, you belong to a rare and small species, rare and small, but not unknown. If you have read all these books, read them again. What makes them great is, among other things, that they teach you something every time you read them. Every time, you see something you had not seen before; you understand something you had missed; no matter how hard your mind worked before, it works again.

And this is the point: every man's mind ought to keep working all his life long; every man's imagination should be touched as often as possible by the great works of imagination; every man ought to push toward the horizons of his intellectual powers all the time. It is impossible to have "had" a liberal education, except in a formal, accidental, immaterial sense. Liberal education ought to end only with life itself.

I must reiterate that you can set no store by your education in childhood and youth, no matter how good it was. Childhood and youth are no time to get an education. They are the time to get ready to get an education. The most that we can hope for from these uninteresting and chaotic periods of life is that during them we shall be set on the right path, the path of realizing our human possibilities through intellectual effort and aesthetic appreciation. The great issues, now issues of life and death for civilization, call for mature minds.

There is a simple test of this. Take any great book that you read in school or college and have not read since. Read it again. Your impression that you understood it will at once be corrected. Think what it means, for instance, to read *Macbeth* at sixteen in contrast to reading it at thirty-five. We can understand *Macbeth* as Shakespeare meant us to understand it only when we have had some experience, vicarious or otherwise, of marriage and ambition. To read great books, if we read them at all, in childhood and youth and never read them again is never to understand them.

Can you ever understand them? There is a sense in which nobody can. That is why the Great Conversation never ends. Jean Cocteau said that each great work in Western thought arises as a contradiction of one that precedes it. This is not the result of the perversity or vanity of these writers. Nobody can make so clear and comprehensive and accurate a statement of the basic issues of human life as to close the discussion. Every statement calls for explanation, correction, modification, expansion, or contradiction.

76

There is, too, the infinite suggestiveness of great books. They lead us to other books, other thoughts, other questions. They enlarge the fund of ideas we have and relate themselves to those we possess. Since the suggestiveness of great books is infinite, we cannot get to the end of them. We cannot say we understand these books in the sense that we are finished with them and what they have to teach us.

The question for you is only whether you can ever understand these books well enough to participate in the Great Conversation, not whether you can understand them well enough to end it. And the answer is that you can never know until you try. We have built up around the "classics" such an atmosphere of pedantry, we have left them so long to the scholarly dissectors, that we think of them as incomprehensible to the ordinary man to whom they were originally addressed. At the same time our education has undergone so drastic a process of dilution that we are ill-equipped, even after graduation from a respectable college, to tackle anything much above the level of the comic book.

The decay of education in the West, which is felt most profoundly in America, undoubtedly makes the task of understanding these books more difficult than it was for earlier generations. In fact my observation leads me to the horrid suspicion that these books are easier for people who have had no formal education than they are for those who have acquired that combination of misinformation, unphilosophy, and slipshod habits that is the usual result of the most elaborate and expensive institutional education in America.

For one thing, those who have had no formal education are less likely to labor under prejudices about the writers contained in this set. They have not heard, or at least not so often, that these authors are archaic, unrealistic and incomprehensible. They approach the books as they would approach any others, with a much more open mind than their more sophisticated, or more miseducated, contemporaries. They have not been frightened by their education.

If you will pick up any one of these books and start to read it, you will find it not nearly so formidable as you thought. In one way the great books are the most difficult, and in another way the easiest, books for any of us to read. They are the most difficult because they deal with the most difficult problems that men can face, and they deal with them in terms of the most complex ideas. But, treating the most difficult subjects of human thought, the great books are the clearest and simplest expression of the best thinking that can be done on these subjects. On the fundamental problems of mankind, there are no easier books to read. If you will pick up any other, after you have read the first, you will find that you understand the second more easily than you did the first and the first better than you did before. The criteria for choosing each book in this set were excellence of construction and composition, immediate intelligibility on the aesthetic level, increasing intelligibility with deeper reading and analysis, leading to maximum depth and maximum range of significance with more than one level of meaning and truth.

In our colleges the curriculum is often so arranged that taking one course is made prerequisite to taking another. The pedagogical habit ingrained by such arrangements may prompt the question: What reading is prerequisite to reading great books? The answer is simply None. For the understanding of great books it is not necessary to read background materials or secondary works about them. But there is one sense in which the reading of a great book may involve prerequisite reading. Except for Homer, the authors of great books who come later in the course of the Great Conversation enter into it themselves as a result of reading the earlier authors. Thus, Plato is a reader of the Homeric poems and of the tragedies and comedies; and Aristotle is a reader of all of these and Plato, too. Dante and Montaigne are readers of most of the Greek and Roman books, not only the poetry and history, but the science and philosophy as well. John Stuart Mill, Karl Marx, William James, and Sigmund Freud are readers of almost all the books in this set.

This suggests that we, as readers of a particular great book, can be helped in reading it by reading first some of the books its author read before writing it. The chronological order of the works in this set is a good reading order precisely because earlier books are in a way the prerequisite reading for later books.

But though earlier books prepare for later ones, it is also true that reading one great book makes reading another easier, no matter in what order they are read. Though earlier books contribute to the education of the authors of later ones, the later authors do more than reflect this influence. They also comment on and interpret the meaning of the earlier works; they report and take issue with the opinions of their predecessors. Looked at forward or backward in the time-sequence, one great book throws light on another; and as the number of great books one has read in any order increases, the voices in the Great Conversation tend more and more to speak in the present tense, as if all the authors were contemporaneous with one another, responding directly to each other's thought.

It takes imaginative and intellectual work to read a book, and facility and achievement grow by exercise. In this set each book is readable ultimately because of its place in the tradition. These books are aware of and responsive to other books, to those which come after them as well as to those which came before. Any good book that is not in the set should be able to find itself subsumed under and related to these great books. Any man should be able, perhaps with some

79

effort, to find his own mind belonging to the discourse in these books. Some degree of understanding of these books should convince you that you are able to read and understand progressively any good book, and to criticize with integrity and security anything written for publication. These books are genuinely intelligible, perhaps late and with difficulty, but ultimately and intrinsically.

Do you need a liberal education? We say that it is unpatriotic not to read these books. You may reply that you are patriotic enough without them. We say that you are gravely cramping your human possibilities if you do not read these books. You may answer that you have troubles enough already.

This answer is the one that Ortega attacks in *The Revolt of the Masses*. It assumes that we can leave all intellectual activity, and all political responsibility, to somebody else and live our lives as vegetable beneficiaries of the moral and intellectual virtue of other men. The trouble with this assumption is that, whereas it was once possible, and even compulsory, for the bulk of mankind, such indulgence now, on the part of anybody, endangers the whole community. It is now necessary for everybody to try to live, as Ortega says, "at the height of his times." The democratic enterprise is imperiled if any one of us says, "I do not have to try to think for myself, or make the most of myself, or become a citizen of the world republic of learning." The death of democracy is not likely to be an assassination from ambush. It will be a slow extinction from apathy, indifference, and undernourishment.

The reply that Edmund Burke gave to the movement for the extension of the suffrage is the one that the majority of men unconsciously supports. Burke developed the doctrine of "virtual representation," which enabled him to claim that all power should reside in the hands of the few, in his case in the hands of the landed aristocracy. They had the qualifications for governing: intelligence, leisure, patriotism, and education. They "virtually" represented the rest of the community, even though the rest of the community had not chosen them to do so. Burke was not interested in the education of the people, because, though government was to be conducted in their interest, it was unthinkable that they could determine what their interest was. They had neither the information, the intelligence, nor the time to govern themselves. "I have often endeavoured," he says, "to compute and to class those who, in any political view are to be called the people. . . . In England and Scotland, I compute that those of adult age, not declining in life, of tolerable leisure for such discussions, and of some means of information, and who are above menial dependence (or what virtually is such), may amount to about four hundred thousand." At that time the population of the British Isles was between eight and ten million.

This is indeed the only reply that can be made to the demand for universal suffrage. It is an attack, and a direct one, on the essential principle of democracy. The virtual representatives of the people are, in Burke's view, in no sense accountable to them. They are responsible to their own consciences, and perhaps to God. But the only way in which the people could call their virtual representatives to time would be through revolution, a prospect that Burke would be the first to deprecate. In his view only those in possession of power are in a position to decide whether or not they should have it. On this principle any totalitarian dictatorship can justify itself.

Dramatically opposed to a position such as that of Burke is the American faith in democracy, and in education in relation to democracy, stated succinctly by Jefferson: "I know of no safe depository of the ultimate powers of society but the people themselves; and if we think them not enlightened enough to exercise their control with a wholesome discretion, the remedy is not to take it from them, but to inform their discretion by education."

We who say, then, that we believe in democracy cannot content ourselves with virtual education any more than we can with virtual representation. We have not the option of deciding for ourselves whether or not we shall be liberal artists, because we are committed to the proposition that all men shall be free. We cannot admit that ordinary people cannot have a good education, because we cannot agree that democracy must involve a degradation of the human ideal. Anything less than the effort to help everybody get the best education necessarily implies that some cannot achieve in their own measure our human ideal. We cannot concede that the conquest of nature, the conquest of drudgery, and the conquest of political power must lead in combination to triviality in education and hence in all the other occupations of life. The aim of education is wisdom, and each must have the chance to become as wise as he can.

POSSIBLE APPROACHES TO THIS SET

POSSIBLE APPROACHES TO THIS SET

FOR REASONS that have been given, the Editors decided against any prefaces or explanatory apparatus in the several volumes of this set. The decision was made to let the great books speak for themselves. The Editors believe that the great books do not need explanation in order to be comprehended by the ordinary reader.

But the ordinary reader, considering the set as a whole, may well ask where he should begin reading and how he should proceed. The Editors have several suggestions to offer.

The first suggestion is a reminder that the *Syntopicon*, which comprises Volumes 2 and 3, provides one kind of answer to the question about where to start and where to go in the reading of the set as a whole. The *Syntopicon* invites the reader to make on the set whatever demands arise from his own problems and interests. It is constructed to enable the reader, no matter what the stages of his reading in other ways, to find that part of the Great Conversation in which any topic that interests him is being discussed.

As explained in the Preface to the *Syntopicon*, its 2,987 topics are organized under 102 basic ideas, to each of which a chapter is devoted; particular topics can also be located by reference to the 1,798 key terms listed in the Inventory of Terms (Volume 3, pp. 1303–1345). When the reader has located the topic of his interest, the *Syntopicon* shows him how to follow the discussion of it that occurs in the twenty-five centuries of the Great Conversation. The Preface to the *Syntopicon* (Volume 2, pp. xi–xxxi) further explains its structure and describes the various uses to which it can be put as a guide to the contents of this set as a whole.

THE GREAT CONVERSATION

The *Syntopicon* helps the reader to begin reading *in* the great books on any subject or subjects in which he is interested, and to follow one idea or one theme through the books from beginning to end. Such syntopical reading *in* the set as a whole, for its varied discourse on a particular theme, supplements the gradual reading of the books taken as individual wholes. Valuable in itself, syntopical reading should bring the reader to an acquaintance with the whole set and thus prepare him to select the particular books he will wish to start reading as wholes.

Yet, apart from the help he will get from syntopical reading, the ordinary reader may still ask with what book he should begin and in what order he should proceed to read the works in this set. One answer is, of course, that he can begin at the beginning, or with any book that especially interests him, and go where the books themselves will lead him. As parts of the Great Conversation, one book naturally leads to another both forward and backward in the time-sequence; each book also leads to many others that deal with the same subject or have some affinity in style or treatment.

If the reader wishes to concentrate for a time on books dealing with one subject matter or with books of a certain kind, such as poetry, history, philosophy, or science, he will find some guidance in the colors in which the books are bound. The volumes bound in *yellow* contain epic and dramatic poetry, satires, and novels. Those bound in *blue* contain histories and works in ethics, economics, politics, and jurisprudence. Those bound in *green* contain mathematics and the natural sciences—works in astronomy, physics, chemistry, biology, and psychology. Those bound in *red* contain philosophy and theology.

Since the individual volumes often include many works by a single author, and sometimes the works of several authors, the classification of the volumes according to the kinds or subject matters indicated above could not always be an adequate representation of their contents. Each volume is placed in one or another of the four large groupings in terms of the predominant character of an author's work. But the works of certain authors cross the line of this or any other simple classification, and certain authors contribute major works in a variety of fields.

For example, Volume 53, which contains William James' *Principles of Psychology*, is grouped with works in natural science, but it also deserves to be considered as a contribution to philosophy. Volumes 7, 8, and 9, which contain the writings of Plato and Aristotle, or Volumes 19, 20, 31, 33, 42, and 46, which contain the writings of Aquinas, Descartes, Pascal, Kant, and Hegel, are classified as philosophy and theology because that accords with the predominant character of their authors, but among the writings that these volumes contain are works in moral and political science, in jurisprudence, in mathematics, in physics, and in biology.

The color of the binding, therefore, serves only as a rough indication of the grouping of the authors and the works according to their literary character or their subject matter. For a more precise selection of individual works of a certain sort, the reader must consult the actual titles of the works that comprise *Great Books of the Western World.* With few exceptions, they plainly indicate the character of the works they name.

To aid the reader in making this selection for himself, if he wishes to concentrate on one subject matter or one kind of book, the Editors have provided on pages 93-110 a complete enumeration, volume by volume, of the full titles of all the works included in *Great Books of the Western World.*

Still another suggestion can be offered in response to the question about the order of reading the books. The Editors have used these books for many years in teaching young people and in leading discussions with groups of adults. They have found that reading whole works or integral parts of works in chronological order and in an ascending scale of difficulty is an effective way of going through the books. This plan has been widely used in the reading courses in great books that are now conducted by some colleges and universities and by the Great Books Foundation in its program of liberal education for adults. It is a plan that is equally good for individual reading.

This plan of reading for this set is set forth on pages 112-131. It consists of reading lists for ten successive years. In their general pattern, these reading lists resemble the lists that have been tried and tested by the Great Books Foundation. But they differ in many particulars, largely as a result of the fact that works that are included in the present lists were not procurable or readily available until the publication of *Great Books of the Western World.*

In this ten-year plan of reading there are eighteen selections for each year, and for each selection the reader is given, in addition to author and title, the volume and page numbers that quickly locate the selection in this set of books.

The selections in each list follow, with one exception, the order of the volumes. That one exception occurs in the first-year list, where Plato's *Apology* and *Crito* (in Volume 7) were placed before Aristophanes' *Clouds* and *Lysistrata* (in Volume 5) because these dialogues of Plato constitute so excellent an introduction to the Great Conversation. The arrangement of the selections according to the order of the volumes in which they are to be found places the readings recommended in each list in the chronological order of the Great Conversation itself. Again, there are a few exceptions that result from the fact that some volumes in the set, in which several authors are grouped together, contain writings that are one or more centuries apart in time.

Each list includes a wide variety of books—almost always poetry, history, and morals or politics, as well as theology, philosophy, and science. The 180 selections recommended in the ten lists represent every author included in *Great Books of the Western World*, though they by no means exhaust the contents of this set. For certain authors, notably the poets and the novelists, the recommended readings cover all their work here published; but for other authors, the selections are only a fair sampling of the range and variety of their contributions to the Great Conversation. Because the brevity of the selections was one consideration in the construction of these lists, especially in the early years, it was necessary to recommend, in the case of certain long works, the reading of successive portions in successive years. But whenever the parts of a single work are divided among several years, or whenever different works by the same author are placed in successive years, the selections are so arranged that the reader is carried through a particular book or through a number of works in an order that accords with the structure of the book or the relation of the works.

Each list has several centers of interest or several connecting themes. Each list represents several phases of the Great Conversation. The lists get more difficult from year to year in two ways. The selections get longer, and they deal with more difficult subject matters. The list for the tenth year, for example, assumes that the reader has completed the reading sug-

88

gested for the other nine, and that the reading he has already engaged in and the books he has already read afford him a certain facility and background for understanding the selections in the tenth year.

The reader who completes this ten-year program will have become acquainted with the range and depth of the Great Conversation. Completing a program of this sort, he will have read, in whole or part, all the authors, though not all the works of every author. He will have a sense of the relations of the authors to one another and of the variety and relations of the ideas with which they deal. He will be in a position to take part in the Great Conversation and should be able to carry his reading of great books on for the rest of his life under the direction of his own interests.

I: The Contents of
Great Books of the Western World

THE CONTENTS OF
GREAT BOOKS OF THE WESTERN WORLD

VOLUME 1
THE GREAT CONVERSATION: *THE SUBSTANCE OF A LIBERAL EDUCATION*

VOLUME 2
THE GREAT IDEAS, *A SYNTOPICON OF GREAT BOOKS OF THE WESTERN WORLD* [I. Angel *to* Love]

VOLUME 3
THE GREAT IDEAS, *A SYNTOPICON OF GREAT BOOKS OF THE WESTERN WORLD* [II. Man *to* World; Bibliography of Additional Readings; Inventory of Terms]

VOLUME 4
HOMER, *THE ILIAD · THE ODYSSEY*

VOLUME 5
AESCHYLUS (*c.* 525–456 B.C.)

THE SUPPLIANT MAIDENS   *PROMETHEUS BOUND*
THE PERSIANS   *AGAMEMNON*
THE SEVEN AGAINST THEBES   *CHOEPHOROE*
EUMENIDES

SOPHOCLES (*c.* 495–406 B.C.)

OEDIPUS THE KING   *AJAX*
OEDIPUS AT COLONUS   *ELECTRA*
ANTIGONE   *TRACHINIAE*
PHILOCTETES

EURIPIDES (*c.* 480–406 B.C.)

RHESUS	*ELECTRA*
MEDEA	*THE BACCHANTES*
HIPPOLYTUS	*HECUBA*
ALCESTIS	*HERACLES MAD*
HERACLEIDAE	*THE PHOENICIAN MAIDENS*
THE SUPPLIANTS	*ORESTES*
THE TROJAN WOMEN	*IPHIGENIA AMONG THE*
ION	*TAURI*
HELEN	*IPHIGENIA AT AULIS*
ANDROMACHE	*THE CYCLOPS*

ARISTOPHANES (*c.* 445–*c.* 380 B.C.)

THE ACHARNIANS	*THE BIRDS*
THE KNIGHTS	*THE FROGS*
THE CLOUDS	*THE LYSISTRATA*
THE WASPS	*THE THESMOPHORIAZUSAE*
THE PEACE	*THE ECCLESIAZUSAE*
	THE PLUTUS

VOLUME 6

HERODOTUS (*c.* 484–*c.*425 B.C.), *THE HISTORY*

THUCYDIDES (*c.* 460–*c.* 400 B.C.), *THE HISTORY OF THE PELOPON-
NESIAN WAR*

VOLUME 7

PLATO (*c.*428–*c.* 348 B.C.)

CHARMIDES	*SYMPOSIUM*
LYSIS	*MENO*
LACHES	*EUTHYPHRO*
PROTAGORAS	*APOLOGY*
EUTHYDEMUS	*CRITO*
CRATYLUS	*PHAEDO*
PHAEDRUS	*GORGIAS*
ION	*THE REPUBLIC*

CONTENTS OF GREAT BOOKS

TIMAEUS   *SOPHIST*

CRITIAS   *STATESMAN*

PARMENIDES   *PHILEBUS*

THEAETETUS   *LAWS*

THE SEVENTH LETTER

VOLUME 8

ARISTOTLE (384–322 B.C.)

CATEGORIES · ON INTERPRETATION

PRIOR ANALYTICS · POSTERIOR ANALYTICS · TOPICS

ON SOPHISTICAL REFUTATIONS · PHYSICS

ON THE HEAVENS · ON GENERATION AND CORRUPTION

METEOROLOGY · METAPHYSICS · ON THE SOUL

ON SENSE AND THE SENSIBLE

ON MEMORY AND REMINISCENCE

ON SLEEP AND SLEEPLESSNESS

ON DREAMS · ON PROPHESYING BY DREAMS

ON LONGEVITY AND SHORTNESS OF LIFE

ON YOUTH AND OLD AGE, ON LIFE AND DEATH,

ON BREATHING

VOLUME 9

ARISTOTLE

HISTORY OF ANIMALS · ON THE PARTS OF ANIMALS

ON THE MOTION OF ANIMALS · ON THE GAIT OF ANIMALS

ON THE GENERATION OF ANIMALS

NICOMACHEAN ETHICS · POLITICS

THE ATHENIAN CONSTITUTION

RHETORIC · ON POETICS

THE GREAT CONVERSATION
VOLUME 10

HIPPOCRATES (*fl.* 400 B.C.)
THE OATH · ON ANCIENT MEDICINE
ON AIRS, WATERS, AND PLACES · THE BOOK OF PROGNOSTICS
ON REGIMEN IN ACUTE DISEASES · OF THE EPIDEMICS
ON INJURIES OF THE HEAD · ON THE SURGERY
ON FRACTURES · ON THE ARTICULATIONS
INSTRUMENTS OF REDUCTION · APHORISMS · THE LAW
ON ULCERS · ON FISTULAE · ON HEMORRHOIDS
ON THE SACRED DISEASE

GALEN (*c.* A.D. 130–*c.* 200), *ON THE NATURAL FACULTIES*

VOLUME 11

EUCLID (*fl. c.* 300 B.C.), *THE THIRTEEN BOOKS OF EUCLID'S
ELEMENTS*

ARCHIMEDES (*c.* 287–212 B.C.)
ON THE SPHERE AND CYLINDER
MEASUREMENT OF A CIRCLE   ON CONOIDS AND SPHEROIDS
ON SPIRALS · ON THE EQUILIBRIUM OF PLANES
THE SAND-RECKONER · QUADRATURE OF THE PARABOLA
ON FLOATING BODIES · BOOK OF LEMMAS
THE METHOD TREATING OF MECHANICAL PROBLEMS

APOLLONIUS OF PERGA (*c.* 262–*c.* 200 B.C.), *ON CONIC SECTIONS*
NICOMACHUS OF GERASA (*fl. c.* A.D. 100), *INTRODUCTION TO
ARITHMETIC*

VOLUME 12

LUCRETIUS (*c.* 98–*c.* 55 B.C.), *ON THE NATURE OF THINGS*
EPICTETUS (*c.* A.D. 60–*c.* 138), *THE DISCOURSES*
MARCUS AURELIUS (A.D. 121–180), *THE MEDITATIONS*

CONTENTS OF GREAT BOOKS

VOLUME 13

VIRGIL (70–19 B.C.), *THE ECLOGUES · THE GEORGICS · THE AENEID*

VOLUME 14

PLUTARCH (*c.* A.D. 46–*c.* 120), *THE LIVES OF THE NOBLE GRECIANS AND ROMANS*

<table>
<tr><td>Theseus</td><td>Marcus Cato</td></tr>
<tr><td>Romulus</td><td>Aristides and Marcus Cato</td></tr>
<tr><td>Romulus and Theseus Compared</td><td>Compared</td></tr>
<tr><td>Lycurgus</td><td>Philopoemen</td></tr>
<tr><td>Numa Pompilius</td><td>Flamininus</td></tr>
<tr><td>Lycurgus and Numa Compared</td><td>Flamininus and Philopoemen</td></tr>
<tr><td>Solon</td><td>Compared</td></tr>
<tr><td>Poplicola</td><td>Pyrrhus</td></tr>
<tr><td>Poplicola and Solon Compared</td><td>Caius Marius</td></tr>
<tr><td>Themistocles</td><td>Lysander</td></tr>
<tr><td>Camillus</td><td>Sulla</td></tr>
<tr><td>Pericles</td><td>Lysander and Sulla Compared</td></tr>
<tr><td>Fabius</td><td>Cimon</td></tr>
<tr><td>Fabius and Pericles Compared</td><td>Lucullus</td></tr>
<tr><td>Alcibiades</td><td>Cimon and Lucullus Compared</td></tr>
<tr><td>Coriolanus</td><td>Nicias</td></tr>
<tr><td>Alcibiades and Coriolanus</td><td>Crassus</td></tr>
<tr><td>Compared</td><td>Crassus and Nicias Compared</td></tr>
<tr><td>Timoleon</td><td>Sertorius</td></tr>
<tr><td>Aemilius Paulus</td><td>Eumenes</td></tr>
<tr><td>Aemilius Paulus and Timoleon</td><td>Eumenes and Sertorius Compared</td></tr>
<tr><td>Compared</td><td>Agesilaus</td></tr>
<tr><td>Pelopidas</td><td>Pompey</td></tr>
<tr><td>Marcellus</td><td>Agesilaus and Pompey Compared</td></tr>
<tr><td>Marcellus and Pelopidas</td><td>Alexander</td></tr>
<tr><td>Compared</td><td>Caesar</td></tr>
<tr><td>Aristides</td><td>Phocion</td></tr>
</table>

THE GREAT CONVERSATION

Cato the Younger	*Demetrius*
Agis	*Antony*
Cleomenes	*Antony and Demetrius Compared*
Tiberius Gracchus	*Dion*
Caius Gracchus	*Marcus Brutus*
Caius and Tiberius Gracchus and Agis and Cleomenes Compared	*Brutus and Dion Compared*
	Aratus
Demosthenes	*Artaxerxes*
Cicero	*Galba*
Demosthenes and Cicero Compared	*Otho*

VOLUME 15

P. CORNELIUS TACITUS (*c.* A.D. 55–*c.* 117), *THE ANNALS · THE HISTORIES*

VOLUME 16

PTOLEMY (*c.* A.D. 100–*c.* 178), *THE ALMAGEST*

NICOLAUS COPERNICUS (1473–1543), *ON THE REVOLUTIONS OF THE HEAVENLY SPHERES*

JOHANNES KEPLER (1571–1630), *EPITOME OF COPERNICAN ASTRONOMY* [Book IV–V] · *THE HARMONIES OF THE WORLD* [Book V]

VOLUME 17

PLOTINUS (205–270), *THE SIX ENNEADS*

VOLUME 18

SAINT AUGUSTINE (354–430), *THE CONFESSIONS · THE CITY OF GOD · ON CHRISTIAN DOCTRINE*

VOLUME 19

SAINT THOMAS AQUINAS (*c.* 1225–1274), *SUMMA THEOLOGICA*
Treatise on God (Part I, QQ 1–26)
Treatise on the Trinity (Part I, QQ 27–43)
Treatise on the Creation (Part I, QQ 44–49)

98

CONTENTS OF GREAT BOOKS

Treatise on the Angels (Part I, QQ 50–64)

Treatise on the Work of the Six Days (Part I, QQ 65–74)

Treatise on Man (Part I, QQ 75–102)

Treatise on the Divine Government (Part I, QQ 103–119)

Treatise on the Last End (Part I–II, QQ 1–5)

Treatise on Human Acts (Part I–II, QQ 6–48)

VOLUME 20

SAINT THOMAS AQUINAS, *SUMMA THEOLOGICA* (cont.)

Treatise on Habits (Part I–II, QQ 49–89)

Treatise on Law (Part I–II, QQ 90–108)

Treatise on Grace (Part I–II, QQ 109–114)

Treatise on Faith, Hope and Charity (Part II–II, QQ 1–46)

Treatise on Active and Contemplative Life (Part II–II, QQ 179–182)

Treatise on the States of Life (Part II–II, QQ 183–189)

Treatise on the Incarnation (Part III, QQ 1–26)

Treatise on the Sacraments (Part III, QQ 60–65)

Treatise on the Resurrection (Part III Supplement, QQ 69–86)

Treatise on the Last Things (Part III Supplement, QQ 87–99)

VOLUME 21

DANTE ALIGHIERI (1265–1321), *THE DIVINE COMEDY*

VOLUME 22

GEOFFREY CHAUCER (*c.* 1340–1400)

TROILUS AND CRESSIDA

THE CANTERBURY TALES

The Prologue
The Knight's Tale
The Miller's Prologue
The Miller's Tale
The Reeve's Prologue

The Reeve's Tale
The Cook's Prologue
The Cook's Tale
*Introduction to the Man of Law's
    Prologue*

The Prologue of the Man of Law's Tale
The Tale of the Man of Law
The Wife of Bath's Prologue
The Tale of the Wife of Bath
The Friar's Prologue
The Friar's Tale
The Summoner's Prologue
The Summoner's Tale
The Clerk's Prologue
The Clerk's Tale
The Merchant's Prologue
The Merchant's Tale
Epilogue to the Merchant's Tale
The Squire's Tale
The Words of the Franklin
The Franklin's Prologue
The Franklin's Tale
The Physician's Tale
The Words of the Host
The Prologue of the Pardoner's Tale
The Pardoner's Tale

The Shipman's Prologue
The Shipman's Tale
The Prioress's Prologue
The Prioress's Tale
Prologue to Sir Thopas
Sir Thopas
Prologue to Melibeus
The Tale of Melibeus
The Monk's Prologue
The Monk's Tale
The Prologue of the Nun's Priest's Tale
The Nun's Priest's Tale
Epilogue to the Nun's Priest's Tale
The Second Nun's Prologue
The Second Nun's Tale
The Canon's Yeoman's Prologue
The Canon's Yeoman's Tale
The Manciple's Prologue
The Manciple's Tale
The Parson's Prologue
The Parson's Tale

L'Envoi

VOLUME 23

NICOLÒ MACHIAVELLI (1469–1527), *THE PRINCE*

THOMAS HOBBES (1588–1679), *LEVIATHAN, OR, MATTER, FORM, AND POWER OF A COMMONWEALTH, ECCLESIASTICAL AND CIVIL*

VOLUME 24

FRANÇOIS RABELAIS (c. 1495–1553), *GARGANTUA AND PANTAGRUEL*

CONTENTS OF GREAT BOOKS
VOLUME 25
MICHEL EYQUEM DE MONTAIGNE (1533–1592), *ESSAYS*

That Men by Various Ways Arrive at the Same End

Of Sorrow

That Our Affections Carry Themselves Beyond Us

That the Soul Discharges Her Passions Upon False Objects, Where the True are Wanting

Whether the Governor of a Place Besieged Ought Himself to Go Out to Parley

That the Hour of Parley is Dangerous

That the Intention is Judge of Our Actions

Of Idleness

Of Liars

Of Quick or Slow Speech

Of Prognostications

Of Constancy

The Ceremony of the Interview of Princes

That Men are Justly Punished for Being Obstinate in the Defence of a Fort that is not in Reason to be Defended

Of the Punishment of Cowardice

A Proceeding of Some Ambassadors

Of Fear

That Men are not to Judge of Our Happiness till After Death

That to Study Philosophy is to Learn to Die

Of the Force of Imagination

That the Profit of One Man is the Damage of Another

Of Custom and That We Should Not Easily Change a Law Received

Various Events from the Same Counsel

Of Pedantry

Of the Education of Children

That It is Folly to Measure Truth and Error by Our Own Capacity

Of Friendship

Nine-and-Twenty Sonnets of Estienne de La Boëtie

Of Moderation

Of Cannibals

That a Man is Soberly to Judge of the Divine Ordinances

That We are to Avoid Pleasures, Even at the Expense of Life

That Fortune is Oftentimes Observed to Act by the Rules of Reason

Of One Defect in Our Government

Of the Custom of Wearing Clothes

Of Cato the Younger

That We Laugh and Cry for the Same Thing

Of Solitude

A Consideration Upon Cicero

That the Relish of Good and Evil Depends in a Great Measure Upon the Opinion We Have of Them

THE GREAT CONVERSATION

Not to Communicate a Man's Honour

Of the Inequality Amongst Us

Of Sumptuary Laws

Of Sleep

Of the Battle of Dreux

Of Names

Of the Uncertainty of Our Judgment

Of War-Horses, or Destriers

Of Ancient Customs

Of Democritus and Heraclitus

Of the Vanity of Words

Of the Parsimony of the Ancients

Of a Saying of Caesar

Of Vain Subtleties

Of Smells

Of Prayers

Of Age

Of the Inconstancy of Our Actions

Of Drunkenness

A Custom of the Isle of Cea

To-morrow's a New Day

Of Conscience

Use Makes Perfect

Of Recompenses of Honour

Of the Affection of Fathers to Their
   Children

Of the Arms of the Parthians

Of Books

Of Cruelty

Apology for Raimond de Sebonde

Of Judging of the Death of Another

That the Mind Hinders Itself

That Our Desires are Augmented by
   Difficulty

Of Glory

Of Presumption

Of Giving the Lie

Of Liberty of Conscience

That We Taste Nothing Pure

Against Idleness

Of Posting

Of Ill Means Employed to a Good End

Of the Roman Grandeur

Not to Counterfeit Being Sick

Of Thumbs

Cowardice the Mother of Cruelty

All Things Have Their Season

Of Virtue

Of a Monstrous Child

Of Anger

Defence of Seneca and Plutarch

The Story of Spurina

Observation on the Means to Carry on
   a War According to Julius Caesar

Of Three Good Women

Of the Most Excellent Men

Of the Resemblance of Children to
   Their Fathers

Of Profit and Honesty

Of Repentance

Of Three Commerces

— Of Diversion

CONTENTS OF GREAT BOOKS

Upon Some Verses of Virgil   *Of Vanity*
Of Coaches   *Of Managing the Will*
Of the Inconvenience of Greatness   *Of Cripples*
Of the Art of Conference   *Of Physiognomy*
                    Of Experience

VOLUME 26

WILLIAM SHAKESPEARE (1564–1616)
   THE FIRST PART OF KING HENRY THE SIXTH
   THE SECOND PART OF KING HENRY THE SIXTH
   THE THIRD PART OF KING HENRY THE SIXTH
   THE TRAGEDY OF KING RICHARD THE THIRD
   THE COMEDY OF ERRORS
   TITUS ANDRONICUS
   THE TAMING OF THE SHREW
   THE TWO GENTLEMEN OF VERONA
   LOVE'S LABOUR'S LOST
   ROMEO AND JULIET
   THE TRAGEDY OF KING RICHARD THE SECOND
   A MIDSUMMER-NIGHT'S DREAM
   THE LIFE AND DEATH OF KING JOHN
   THE MERCHANT OF VENICE
   THE FIRST PART OF KING HENRY THE FOURTH
   THE SECOND PART OF KING HENRY THE FOURTH
   MUCH ADO ABOUT NOTHING
   THE LIFE OF KING HENRY THE FIFTH
   JULIUS CAESAR · AS YOU LIKE IT

VOLUME 27

WILLIAM SHAKESPEARE
   TWELFTH NIGHT; OR, WHAT YOU WILL
   HAMLET, PRINCE OF DENMARK

THE GREAT CONVERSATION

THE MERRY WIVES OF WINDSOR
TROILUS AND CRESSIDA
ALL'S WELL THAT ENDS WELL
MEASURE FOR MEASURE
OTHELLO, THE MOOR OF VENICE
KING LEAR · MACBETH
ANTONY AND CLEOPATRA
CORIOLANUS · TIMON OF ATHENS
PERICLES, PRINCE OF TYRE · CYMBELINE
THE WINTER'S TALE · THE TEMPEST
THE FAMOUS HISTORY OF THE LIFE OF
KING HENRY THE EIGHTH
SONNETS

VOLUME 28

WILLIAM GILBERT (1540–1603), *ON THE LOADSTONE AND MAG-NETIC BODIES*

GALILEO GALILEI (1564–1642), *DIALOGUES CONCERNING THE TWO NEW SCIENCES*

WILLIAM HARVEY (1578–1657)
ON THE MOTION OF THE HEART AND BLOOD IN ANIMALS
ON THE CIRCULATION OF THE BLOOD
ON THE GENERATION OF ANIMALS

VOLUME 29

MIGUEL DE CERVANTES (1547–1616), *THE HISTORY OF DON QUIXOTE DE LA MANCHA*

VOLUME 30

SIR FRANCIS BACON (1561–1626), *ADVANCEMENT OF LEARN-ING · NOVUM ORGANUM · NEW ATLANTIS*

CONTENTS OF GREAT BOOKS

VOLUME 31

RENE DESCARTES (1596-1650)
RULES FOR THE DIRECTION OF THE MIND
DISCOURSE ON THE METHOD
MEDITATIONS ON FIRST PHILOSOPHY
OBJECTIONS AGAINST THE MEDITATIONS AND REPLIES
THE GEOMETRY

BENEDICT DE SPINOZA (1632-1677), *ETHICS*

VOLUME 32

JOHN MILTON (1608-1674)
ENGLISH MINOR POEMS

On the Morning of Christs Nativity and *The Hymn*
A Paraphrase on Psalm 114
Psalm 136
The Passion
On Time
Upon the Circumcision
At a Solemn Musick
An Epitaph on the Marchioness of Winchester
Song on May Morning
On Shakespear, 1630
On the University Carrier
Another on the Same
L'Allegro
Il Penseroso

Arcades
Lycidas
Comus
On the Death of a Fair Infant
At a Vacation Exercise
The Fifth Ode of Horace. Lib. I
Sonnets, I, VII-XIX
On the New Forcers of Conscience under the Long Parliament
On the Lord Gen. Fairfax at the siege of Colchester
To the Lord Generall Cromwell May 1652
To Sr Henry Vane the Younger
To Mr. Cyriack Skinner upon his Blindness

Psalms, I-VIII, LXXX-LXXXVIII

PARADISE LOST
SAMSON AGONISTES
AREOPAGITICA

THE GREAT CONVERSATION
VOLUME 33

BLAISE PASCAL (1623–1662)

THE PROVINCIAL LETTERS

PENSEES

PREFACE TO THE TREATISE ON THE VACUUM

NEW EXPERIMENTS CONCERNING THE VACUUM

ACCOUNT OF THE GREAT EXPERIMENT CONCERNING THE EQUILIBRIUM OF FLUIDS

TREATISES ON THE EQUILIBRIUM OF LIQUIDS AND ON THE WEIGHT OF THE MASS OF THE AIR

ON GEOMETRICAL DEMONSTRATION

TREATISE ON THE ARITHMETICAL TRIANGLE

CORRESPONDENCE WITH FERMAT ON THE THEORY OF PROB-ABILITIES

VOLUME 34

SIR ISAAC NEWTON (1642–1727), *MATHEMATICAL PRINCIPLES OF NATURAL PHILOSOPHY · OPTICS*

CHRISTIAAN HUYGENS (1629–1695), *TREATISE ON LIGHT*

VOLUME 35

JOHN LOCKE (1632–1704)

A LETTER CONCERNING TOLERATION

CONCERNING CIVIL GOVERNMENT, SECOND ESSAY

AN ESSAY CONCERNING HUMAN UNDERSTANDING

GEORGE BERKELEY (1685–1753), *THE PRINCIPLES OF HUMAN KNOWLEDGE*

DAVID HUME (1711–1776), *AN ENQUIRY CONCERNING HUMAN UNDERSTANDING*

CONTENTS OF GREAT BOOKS

VOLUME 36

JONATHAN SWIFT (1667–1745), *GULLIVER'S TRAVELS*

LAURENCE STERNE (1713–1768), *THE LIFE AND OPINIONS OF TRISTRAM SHANDY, GENT.*

VOLUME 37

HENRY FIELDING (1707–1754), *THE HISTORY OF TOM JONES, A FOUNDLING*

VOLUME 38

CHARLES DE SECONDAT, BARON DE MONTESQUIEU (1689–1755), *THE SPIRIT OF LAWS*

JEAN JACQUES ROUSSEAU (1712–1778)
A DISCOURSE ON THE ORIGIN OF INEQUALITY
A DISCOURSE ON POLITICAL ECONOMY
THE SOCIAL CONTRACT

VOLUME 39

ADAM SMITH (1723–1790), *AN INQUIRY INTO THE NATURE AND CAUSES OF THE WEALTH OF NATIONS*

VOLUME 40

EDWARD GIBBON (1737–1794), *THE DECLINE AND FALL OF THE ROMAN EMPIRE* [Chapters 1–40]

VOLUME 41

EDWARD GIBBON, *THE DECLINE AND FALL OF THE ROMAN EMPIRE* (Cont.) [Chapters 41–71]

VOLUME 42

IMMANUEL KANT (1724–1804)
THE CRITIQUE OF PURE REASON
FUNDAMENTAL PRINCIPLES OF THE METAPHYSIC OF MORALS

THE GREAT CONVERSATION

THE CRITIQUE OF PRACTICAL REASON
PREFACE AND INTRODUCTION TO THE METAPHYSICAL ELE-
MENTS OF ETHICS WITH A NOTE ON CONSCIENCE
GENERAL INTRODUCTION TO THE METAPHYSIC OF MORALS
THE SCIENCE OF RIGHT
THE CRITIQUE OF JUDGEMENT

VOLUME 43

AMERICAN STATE PAPERS
THE DECLARATION OF INDEPENDENCE
ARTICLES OF CONFEDERATION
THE CONSTITUTION OF THE UNITED STATES OF AMERICA

ALEXANDER HAMILTON (1757–1804), JAMES MADISON (1751–1836), JOHN JAY (1745–1829)
THE FEDERALIST

JOHN STUART MILL (1806–1873)
ON LIBERTY
REPRESENTATIVE GOVERNMENT
UTILITARIANISM

VOLUME 44

JAMES BOSWELL (1740–1795), *THE LIFE OF SAMUEL JOHNSON, LL.D.*

VOLUME 45

ANTOINE LAURENT LAVOISIER (1743–1794), *ELEMENTS OF CHEMISTRY*

JEAN BAPTISTE JOSEPH FOURIER (1768–1830), *ANALYTICAL THEORY OF HEAT* [Preliminary Discourse, Ch. 1–2]

MICHAEL FARADAY (1791–1867), *EXPERIMENTAL RESEARCHES IN ELECTRICITY*

CONTENTS OF GREAT BOOKS

VOLUME 46
GEORG WILHELM FRIEDRICH HEGEL (1770–1831), *THE PHILOS-OPHY OF RIGHT · THE PHILOSOPHY OF HISTORY*

VOLUME 47
JOHANN WOLFGANG von GOETHE (1749–1832), *FAUST*

VOLUME 48
HERMAN MELVILLE (1819–1882), *MOBY DICK; OR, THE WHALE*

VOLUME 49
CHARLES DARWIN (1809–1882)
THE ORIGIN OF SPECIES BY MEANS OF NATURAL SELECTION
THE DESCENT OF MAN AND SELECTION IN RELATION TO SEX

VOLUME 50
KARL MARX (1818–1883), *CAPITAL*

KARL MARX and FRIEDRICH ENGELS (1820–1895), *MANIFESTO OF THE COMMUNIST PARTY*

VOLUME 51
COUNT LEO TOLSTOY (1828–1910), *WAR AND PEACE*

VOLUME 52
FYODOR MIKHAILOVICH DOSTOEVSKY (1821–1881), *THE BROTHERS KARAMAZOV*

VOLUME 53
WILLIAM JAMES (1842–1910), *THE PRINCIPLES OF PSYCHOLOGY*

VOLUME 54
SIGMUND FREUD (1856–1939)
THE ORIGIN AND DEVELOPMENT OF PSYCHO-ANALYSIS
SELECTED PAPERS ON HYSTERIA [Chapters 1–10]
THE SEXUAL ENLIGHTENMENT OF CHILDREN
THE FUTURE PROSPECTS OF PSYCHO-ANALYTIC THERAPY

THE GREAT CONVERSATION

OBSERVATIONS ON "WILD" PSYCHO-ANALYSIS
THE INTERPRETATION OF DREAMS
ON NARCISSISM
INSTINCTS AND THEIR VICISSITUDES
REPRESSION
THE UNCONSCIOUS
A GENERAL INTRODUCTION TO PSYCHO-ANALYSIS
BEYOND THE PLEASURE PRINCIPLE
GROUP PSYCHOLOGY AND THE ANALYSIS OF THE EGO
THE EGO AND THE ID
INHIBITIONS, SYMPTOMS, AND ANXIETY
THOUGHTS FOR THE TIMES ON WAR AND DEATH
CIVILIZATION AND ITS DISCONTENTS
NEW INTRODUCTORY LECTURES ON PSYCHO-ANALYSIS

II: Ten Years of Reading in
Great Books of the Western World

FIRST YEAR

1. PLATO: *APOLOGY, CRITO*
   Vol. 7, pp. 200–219

2. ARISTOPHANES: *CLOUDS, LYSISTRATA*
   Vol. 5, pp. 488–506, 583–599

3. PLATO: *REPUBLIC* [Book I–II]
   Vol. 7, pp. 295–324

4. ARISTOTLE: *ETHICS* [Book I]
   Vol. 9, pp. 339–348

5. ARISTOTLE: *POLITICS* [Book I]
   Vol. 9, pp. 445–455

6. PLUTARCH: *THE LIVES OF THE NOBLE GRECIANS AND ROMANS* [Lycurgus, Numa Pompilius, Lycurgus and Numa Compared, Alexander, Caesar]
   Vol. 14, pp. 32–64, 540–604

7. *NEW TESTAMENT* [The Gospel According to Saint Matthew, The Acts of the Apostles]

8. ST. AUGUSTINE: *CONFESSIONS* [Book I–VIII]
   Vol. 18, pp. 1–61

9. MACHIAVELLI: *THE PRINCE*
   Vol. 23, pp. 1–37

10. RABELAIS: *GARGANTUA AND PANTAGRUEL* [Book I–II]
    Vol. 24, pp. 1–126

11. MONTAIGNE: *ESSAYS* [Of Custom, and That We Should Not Easily Change a Law Received; Of Pedantry; Of the Education of Children; That It Is Folly to Measure Truth and Error by Our Own

Capacity; Of Cannibals; That the Relish of Good and Evil Depends in a Great Measure upon the Opinion We Have of Them; Upon Some Verses of Virgil]

Vol. 25, pp. 42–51, 55–82, 91–98, 115–125, 406–434

12. SHAKESPEARE: *HAMLET*

Vol. 27, pp. 29–72

13. LOCKE: *CONCERNING CIVIL GOVERNMENT* [Second Essay]

Vol. 35, pp. 25–81

14. ROUSSEAU: *THE SOCIAL CONTRACT* [Book I–II]

Vol. 38, pp. 387–406

15. GIBBON: *THE DECLINE AND FALL OF THE ROMAN EMPIRE* [Ch. 15–16]

Vol. 40, pp. 179–234

16. *THE DECLARATION OF INDEPENDENCE, THE CONSTITUTION OF THE UNITED STATES, THE FEDERALIST* [Numbers 1–10, 15, 31, 47, 51, 68–71]

Vol. 43, pp. 1–3, 11–20, 29–53, 62–66, 103–105, 153–156, 162–165, 205–216

17. SMITH: *THE WEALTH OF NATIONS* [Introduction—Book I, Ch. 9]

Vol. 39, pp. 1–41

18. MARX–ENGELS: *MANIFESTO OF THE COMMUNIST PARTY*

, Vol. 50, pp. 415–434

THE GREAT CONVERSATION

SECOND YEAR

1. HOMER: *THE ILIAD*
   Vol. 4, pp. 3–179
2. AESCHYLUS: *AGAMEMNON, CHOEPHOROE, EUMENIDES*
   Vol. 5, pp. 52–91
3. SOPHOCLES: *OEDIPUS THE KING, ANTIGONE*
   Vol. 5, pp. 99–113, 131–142
4. HERODOTUS: *THE HISTORY* [Book I–II]
   Vol. 6, pp. 1–88
5. PLATO: *MENO*
   Vol. 7, pp. 174–190
6. ARISTOTLE: *POETICS*
   Vol. 9, pp. 681–699
7. ARISTOTLE: *ETHICS* [Book II; Book III. Ch. 5–12; Book VI, Ch. 8–13]
   Vol. 9, pp. 348–355, 359–366, 390–394
8. NICOMACHUS: *INTRODUCTION TO ARITHMETIC*
   Vol. 11, pp. 811–848
9. LUCRETIUS: *ON THE NATURE OF THINGS* [Book I-IV]
   Vol. 12, pp. 1–61
10. MARCUS AURELIUS: *MEDITATIONS*
    Vol. 12, pp. 253–310
11. HOBBES: *LEVIATHAN* [Part I]
    Vol. 23, pp. 45–98
12. MILTON: *AREOPAGITICA*
    Vol. 32, pp. 381–412

    114

13. PASCAL: *PENSÉES* [Numbers 72, 82–83, 100, 128, 131, 139, 142–143, 171, 194–195, 219, 229, 233–234, 242, 273, 277, 282, 289, 298, 303, 320, 323, 325, 330–331, 374, 385, 392, 395–397, 409, 412–413, 416, 418, 425, 430, 434–435, 463, 491, 525–531, 538, 543, 547, 553, 556, 564, 571, 586, 598, 607–610, 613, 619–620, 631, 640, 644, 673, 675, 684, 692–693, 737, 760, 768, 792–793]
    Vol. 33, pp. 181–184, 186–189, 191–192, 195–200, 203, 205–210, 212–218, 222–225, 227, 229–232, 237–251, 255, 259, 264–275, 277–287, 290–291, 296–302, 318, 321–322, 326–327

14. PASCAL: *TREATISE ON THE ARITHMETICAL TRIANGLE*
    Vol. 33, pp. 447–473

15. SWIFT: *GULLIVER'S TRAVELS*
    Vol. 36, pp. xv–184

16. ROUSSEAU: *A DISCOURSE ON THE ORIGIN OF INEQUALITY*
    Vol. 38, pp. 323–366

17. KANT: *FUNDAMENTAL PRINCIPLES OF THE METAPHYSIC OF MORALS*
    Vol. 42, pp. 253–287

18. MILL: *ON LIBERTY*
    Vol. 43, pp. 267–323

THIRD YEAR

1. AESCHYLUS: *PROMETHEUS BOUND*
   Vol. 5, pp. 40–51

2. HERODOTUS: *THE HISTORY* [Book VII–IX]
   Vol. 6, pp. 214–314

3. THUCYDIDES: *THE HISTORY OF THE PELOPONNESIAN WAR*
   [Book I–II, V]
   Vol. 6, pp. 349–416, 482–508

4. PLATO: *STATESMAN*
   Vol. 7, pp. 580–608

5. ARISTOTLE: *ON INTERPRETATION* [Ch. 1–10]
   Vol. 8, pp. 25–31

6. ARISTOTLE: *POLITICS* [Book III–V]
   Vol. 9, pp. 471–519

7. EUCLID: *ELEMENTS* [Book I]
   Vol. 11, pp. 1–29

8. TACITUS: *THE ANNALS*
   Vol. 15, pp. 1–184

9. ST. THOMAS AQUINAS: *SUMMA THEOLOGICA* [Part I–II, QQ 90–97]
   Vol. 20, pp. 205–239

10. CHAUCER: *TROILUS AND CRESSIDA*
    Vol. 22, pp. 1–155

11. SHAKESPEARE: *MACBETH*
    Vol. 27, pp. 284–310

12. MILTON: *PARADISE LOST*
    Vol. 32, pp. 93-333
13. LOCKE: *AN ESSAY CONCERNING HUMAN UNDERSTANDING*
    [Book III, Ch. 1-3, 9-11]
    Vol. 35, pp. 251-260, 285-306
14. KANT: *SCIENCE OF RIGHT*
    Vol. 42, pp. 397-458
15. MILL: *REPRESENTATIVE GOVERNMENT* [Ch. 1-6]
    Vol. 43, pp. 327-370
16. LAVOISIER: *ELEMENTS OF CHEMISTRY* [Part I]
    Vol. 45, pp. 1-52
17. DOSTOEVSKY: *THE BROTHERS KARAMAZOV* [Part I-II]
    Vol. 52, pp. 1-170
18. FREUD: *THE ORIGIN AND DEVELOPMENT OF PSYCHO-ANALYSIS*
    Vol. 54, pp. 1-20

FOURTH YEAR

1. EURIPIDES: *MEDEA, HIPPOLYTUS, TROJAN WOMEN, THE BACCHANTES*
   Vol. 5, pp. 212–236, 270–281, 340–352
2. PLATO: *REPUBLIC* [Book VI–VII]
   Vol. 7, pp. 373–401
3. PLATO: *THEAETETUS*
   Vol. 7, pp. 512–550
4. ARISTOTLE: *PHYSICS* [Book IV, Ch. 1–5, 10–14]
   Vol. 8, pp. 287–292, 297–304
5. ARISTOTLE: *METAPHYSICS* [Book I, Ch. 1–2; Book IV; Book VI, Ch. 1; Book XI, Ch. 1–4]
   Vol. 8, pp. 499–501, 522–532, 547–548, 587–590
6. ST. AUGUSTINE: *CONFESSIONS* [Book IX–XIII]
   Vol. 18, pp. 61–125
7. ST. THOMAS AQUINAS: *SUMMA THEOLOGICA* [Part I, QQ 16–17, 84–88]
   Vol. 19, pp. 94–104, 440–473
8. MONTAIGNE: *APOLOGY FOR RAIMOND DE SEBONDE*
   Vol. 25, pp. 208–294
9. GALILEO: *TWO NEW SCIENCES* [Third Day, through Scholium of Theorem II]
   Vol. 28, pp. 197–210
10. BACON: *NOVUM ORGANUM* [Preface, Book I]
    Vol. 30, pp. 105–136
11. DESCARTES: *DISCOURSE ON THE METHOD*
    Vol. 31, pp. 41–67

12. NEWTON: *MATHEMATICAL PRINCIPLES OF NATURAL PHILOSOPHY* [Prefaces, Definitions, Axioms, General Scholium]
    Vol. 34, pp. 1–24, 369–372

13. LOCKE: *AN ESSAY CONCERNING HUMAN UNDERSTANDING* [Book II]
    Vol. 35, pp. 121–251

14. HUME: *AN ENQUIRY CONCERNING HUMAN UNDERSTAND-ING*
    Vol. 35, pp. 450–509

15. KANT: *CRITIQUE OF PURE REASON* [Prefaces, Introduction, Transcendental Aesthetic]
    Vol. 42, pp. 1–33

16. MELVILLE: *MOBY DICK*
    Vol. 48

17. DOSTOEVSKY: *THE BROTHERS KARAMAZOV* [Part III–IV]
    Vol. 52, pp. 171–412

18. JAMES: *PRINCIPLES OF PSYCHOLOGY* [Ch. XV, XX]
    Vol. 53, pp. 396–420, 540–635

FIFTH YEAR

1. PLATO: *PHAEDO*
   Vol. 7, pp. 220–251

2. ARISTOTLE: *CATEGORIES*
   Vol. 8, pp. 5–21

3. ARISTOTLE: *ON THE SOUL* [Book II, Ch. 1–3; Book III]
   Vol. 8, pp. 642–645, 656–668

4. HIPPOCRATES: *THE OATH; ON ANCIENT MEDICINE; ON AIRS, WATERS, AND PLACES; THE BOOK OF PROGNOSTICS; OF THE EPIDEMICS; THE LAW; ON THE SACRED DISEASE*
   Vol. 10, pp. xiii–26, 44–63, 144, 154–160

5. GALEN: *ON THE NATURAL FACULTIES*
   Vol. 10, pp. 167–215

6. VIRGIL: *THE AENEID*
   Vol. 13, pp. 103–379

7. PTOLEMY: *THE ALMAGEST* [Book I, Ch. 1–8]
   COPERNICUS: *REVOLUTIONS OF THE HEAVENLY SPHERES* [Introduction—Book I, Ch. 11]
   KEPLER: *EPITOME OF COPERNICAN ASTRONOMY* [Book IV, Part II, Ch. 1–2]
   Vol. 16, pp. 5–14, 505–532, 887–895

8. PLOTINUS: *SIXTH ENNEAD*
   Vol. 17, pp. 252–360

9. ST. THOMAS AQUINAS: *SUMMA THEOLOGICA* [Part I, QQ 75–76, 78–79]
   Vol. 19, pp. 378–399, 407–427

10. DANTE: *THE DIVINE COMEDY* [Hell]
    Vol. 21, pp. 1–52

11. HARVEY: *THE MOTION OF THE HEART AND BLOOD*
    Vol. 28, pp. 267–304

12. CERVANTES: *DON QUIXOTE* [Part I]
    Vol. 29, pp. xi–204

13. SPINOZA: *ETHICS* [Part II]
    Vol. 31, pp. 373–394

14. BERKELEY: *THE PRINCIPLES OF HUMAN KNOWLEDGE*
    Vol. 35, pp. 403–444

15. KANT: *CRITIQUE OF PURE REASON* [Transcendental Analytic]
    Vol. 42, pp. 34–108

16. DARWIN: *THE ORIGIN OF SPECIES* [Introduction—Ch. 6, Ch. 15]
    Vol. 49, pp. 6–98, 230–243

17. TOLSTOY: *WAR AND PEACE* [Book I–VIII]
    Vol. 51, pp. 1–341

18. JAMES: *PRINCIPLES OF PSYCHOLOGY* [Ch. XXVIII]
    Vol. 53, pp. 851–897

SIXTH YEAR

1. *OLD TESTAMENT* [Genesis, Exodus, Deuteronomy]
2. HOMER: *THE ODYSSEY*
     Vol. 4, pp. 183–322
3. PLATO: *LAWS* [Book X]
     Vol. 7, pp. 757–771
4. ARISTOTLE: *METAPHYSICS* [Book XII]
     Vol. 8, pp. 598–606
5. TACITUS: *THE HISTORIES*
     Vol. 15, pp. 189–302
6. PLOTINUS: *FIFTH ENNEAD*
     Vol. 17, pp. 208–251
7. ST. AUGUSTINE: *THE CITY OF GOD* [Book XV–XVIII]
     Vol. 18, pp. 397–507
8. ST. THOMAS AQUINAS: *SUMMA THEOLOGICA* [Part I, QQ 1–13]
     Vol. 19, pp. 3–75
9. DANTE: *THE DIVINE COMEDY* [Purgatory]
     Vol. 21, pp. 53–105
10. SHAKESPEARE: *COMEDY OF ERRORS, THE TAMING OF THE SHREW, AS YOU LIKE IT, TWELFTH NIGHT*
     Vol. 26, pp. 149–169, 199–228, 597–626; Vol. 27, pp. 1–28
11. SPINOZA: *ETHICS* [Part I]
     Vol. 31, pp. 355–372
12. MILTON: *SAMSON AGONISTES*
     Vol. 32, pp. 337–378

13. PASCAL: *THE PROVINCIAL LETTERS*
    Vol. 33, pp. 1–167

14. LOCKE: *AN ESSAY CONCERNING HUMAN UNDERSTANDING*
    [Book IV]
    Vol. 35, pp. 307–395

15. GIBBON: *THE DECLINE AND FALL OF THE ROMAN EMPIRE*
    [Ch. 1–5, General Observations on the Fall of the Roman Empire
    in the West]
    Vol. 40, pp. 1–51, 630–634

16. KANT: *CRITIQUE OF PURE REASON* [Transcendental Dialectic]
    Vol. 42, pp. 108–209

17. HEGEL: *PHILOSOPHY OF HISTORY* [Introduction]
    Vol. 46, pp. 153–206

18. TOLSTOY: *WAR AND PEACE* [Book IX–XV, Epilogues]
    Vol. 51, pp. 342–696

SEVENTH YEAR

1. *OLD TESTAMENT* [Job, Isaiah, Amos]
2. PLATO: *SYMPOSIUM*
   Vol. 7, pp. 149–173
3. PLATO: *PHILEBUS*
   Vol. 7, pp. 609–639
4. ARISTOTLE: *ETHICS* [Book VIII–X]
   Vol. 9, pp. 406–436
5. ARCHIMEDES: *MEASUREMENT OF A CIRCLE, THE EQUI-
   LIBRIUM OF PLANES* [Book I], *THE SAND-RECKONER, ON
   FLOATING BODIES* [Book I]
   Vol. 11, pp. 447–451, 502–509, 520–526, 538–542
6. EPICTETUS: *DISCOURSES*
   Vol. 12, pp. 105–245
7. PLOTINUS: *FIRST ENNEAD*
   Vol. 17, pp. 1–34
8. ST. THOMAS AQUINAS: *SUMMA THEOLOGICA* [Part I–II, QQ
   1–5]
   Vol. 19, pp. 609–643
9. DANTE: *THE DIVINE COMEDY* [Paradise]
   Vol. 21, pp. 106–157
10. RABELAIS: *GARGANTUA AND PANTAGRUEL* [Book III–IV]
    Vol. 24, pp. 127–312
11. SHAKESPEARE: *JULIUS CAESAR, ANTONY AND CLEOPA-
    TRA, CORIOLANUS*
    Vol. 26, pp. 568–596; Vol. 27, pp. 311–392

12. GALILEO: *TWO NEW SCIENCES* [First Day]
    Vol. 28, pp. 131–177

13. SPINOZA: *ETHICS* [Part IV–V]
    Vol. 31, pp. 422–463

14. NEWTON: *MATHEMATICAL PRINCIPLES OF NATURAL PHILOSOPHY* [Book III, Rules], *OPTICS* [Book I, Part I; Book III, Queries]
    Vol. 34, pp. 270–271, 379–423, 516–544

15. HUYGENS: *TREATISE ON LIGHT*
    Vol. 34, pp. 551–619

16. KANT: *CRITIQUE OF PRACTICAL REASON*
    Vol. 42, pp. 291–361

17. KANT: *CRITIQUE OF JUDGEMENT* [Critique of Aesthetic Judgement]
    Vol. 42, pp. 461–549

18. MILL: *UTILITARIANISM*
    Vol. 43, pp. 445–476

EIGHTH YEAR

1. ARISTOPHANES: *THESMOPHORIAZUSAE, ECCLESIAZUSAE, PLUTUS*
   Vol. 5, pp. 600–642

2. PLATO: *GORGIAS*
   Vol. 7, pp. 252–294

3. ARISTOTLE: *ETHICS* [Book V]
   Vol. 9, pp. 376–387

4. ARISTOTLE: *RHETORIC* [Book I, Ch. 1—Book II, Ch. 1; Book II, Ch. 20—Book III, Ch. 1; Book III, Ch. 13–19]
   Vol. 9, pp. 593–623, 640–654, 667–675

5. ST. AUGUSTINE: *ON CHRISTIAN DOCTRINE*
   Vol. 18, pp. 619–698

6. HOBBES: *LEVIATHAN* [Part II]
   Vol. 23, pp. 99–164

7. SHAKESPEARE: *OTHELLO, KING LEAR*
   Vol. 27, pp. 205–283

8. BACON: *ADVANCEMENT OF LEARNING* [Book I, Ch. 1—Book II, Ch. 11]
   Vol. 30, pp. 1–55

9. DESCARTES: *MEDITATIONS ON THE FIRST PHILOSOPHY*
   Vol. 31, pp. 69–103

10. SPINOZA: *ETHICS* [Part III]
    Vol. 31, pp. 395–422

11. LOCKE: *A LETTER CONCERNING TOLERATION*
    Vol. 35, pp. 1–22

12. STERNE: *TRISTRAM SHANDY*
    Vol. 36, pp. 190–556
13. ROUSSEAU: *A DISCOURSE ON POLITICAL ECONOMY*
    Vol. 38, pp. 367–385
14. ADAM SMITH: *THE WEALTH OF NATIONS* [Book II]
    Vol. 39, pp. 117–162
15. BOSWELL: *THE LIFE OF SAMUEL JOHNSON*
    Vol. 44, pp. 49–55, 104–139, 159–173, 247–262, 281–322
16. MARX: *CAPITAL* [Prefaces, Part I–II]
    Vol. 50, pp. 1–84
17. GOETHE: *FAUST* [Part I]
    Vol. 47, pp. 1–114
18. JAMES: *PRINCIPLES OF PSYCHOLOGY* [Ch. VIII–X]
    Vol. 53, pp. 130–259

NINTH YEAR

1. PLATO: *THE SOPHIST*
   Vol. 7, pp. 551–579

2. THUCYDIDES: *THE HISTORY OF THE PELOPONNESIAN WAR* [Book VII–VIII]
   Vol. 6, pp. 538–593

3. ARISTOTLE: *POLITICS* [Book VII–VIII]
   Vol. 9, pp. 527–548

4. APOLLONIUS: *ON CONIC SECTIONS* [Book I, Prop. 1–15; Book III, Prop. 42–55]
   Vol. 11, pp. 603–624, 780–797

5. *NEW TESTAMENT* [The Gospel According to Saint John, The Epistle of Paul the Apostle to the Romans, The First Epistle of Paul the Apostle to the Corinthians]

6. ST. AUGUSTINE: *THE CITY OF GOD* [Book V, XIX]
   Vol. 18, pp. 207–230, 507–530

7. ST. THOMAS AQUINAS: *SUMMA THEOLOGICA* [Part II–II, QQ 1–7]
   Vol. 20, pp. 380–416

8. GILBERT: *ON THE LOADSTONE*
   Vol. 28, pp. 1–121

9. DESCARTES: *RULES FOR THE DIRECTION OF THE MIND*
   Vol. 31, pp. 1–40

10. DESCARTES: *GEOMETRY*
    Vol. 31, pp. 295–353

11. PASCAL: *THE GREAT EXPERIMENT CONCERNING THE EQUI-
    LIBRIUM OF FLUIDS, ON GEOMETRICAL DEMONSTRATION*
      Vol. 33, pp. 382–389, 430–446

12. FIELDING: *TOM JONES*
      Vol. 37

13. MONTESQUIEU: *THE SPIRIT OF LAWS* [Book I–V, VIII, XI–
    XII]
      Vol. 38, pp. 1–33, 51–58, 68–96

14. FOURIER: *ANALYTICAL THEORY OF HEAT* [Preliminary
    Discourse, Ch. 1-2]
      Vol. 45, pp. 169–251

15. FARADAY: *EXPERIMENTAL RESEARCHES IN ELECTRICITY*
    [Series I–II], *A SPECULATION TOUCHING ELECTRIC CON-
    DUCTION AND THE NATURE OF MATTER*
      Vol. 45, pp. 265–302, 850–855

16. HEGEL: *PHILOSOPHY OF RIGHT* [Part III]
      Vol. 46, pp. 55–114

17. MARX: *CAPITAL* [Part III–IV]
      Vol. 50, pp. 85–250

18. FREUD: *CIVILIZATION AND ITS DISCONTENTS*
      Vol. 54, pp. 767–802

TENTH YEAR

1. SOPHOCLES: *AJAX, ELECTRA*
   Vol. 5, pp. 143–169

2. PLATO: *TIMAEUS*
   Vol. 7, pp. 442–477

3. ARISTOTLE: *ON THE PARTS OF ANIMALS* [Book I, Ch. 1—
   Book II, Ch. 1], *ON THE GENERATION OF ANIMALS* [Book I,
   Ch. 1, 17–18, 20–23]
   Vol. 9, pp. 161–171, 255–256, 261–266, 268–271

4. LUCRETIUS: *ON THE NATURE OF THINGS* [Book V–VI]
   Vol. 12, pp. 61–97

5. VIRGIL: *THE ECLOGUES, THE GEORGICS*
   Vol. 13, pp. 3–99

6. ST. THOMAS AQUINAS: *SUMMA THEOLOGICA* [Part I, QQ
   65–74]
   Vol. 19, pp. 339–377

7. ST. THOMAS AQUINAS: *SUMMA THEOLOGICA* [Part I, QQ
   90–102]
   Vol. 19, pp. 480–527

8. CHAUCER: *CANTERBURY TALES* [Prologue, Knight's Tale,
   Miller's Prologue and Tale, Reeve's Prologue and Tale, Wife of
   Bath's Prologue and Tale, Friar's Prologue and Tale, Summoner's
   Prologue and Tale, Pardoner's Prologue and Tale]
   Vol. 22, pp. 159–232, 256–295, 372–382

130

9. SHAKESPEARE: *THE TRAGEDY OF KING RICHARD II, THE FIRST PART OF KING HENRY IV, THE SECOND PART OF KING HENRY IV, THE LIFE OF KING HENRY V*
   Vol. 26, pp. 320–351, 434–502, 532–567

10. HARVEY: *ON THE GENERATION OF ANIMALS* [Introduction —Exercise 62]
    Vol. 28, pp. 331–470

11. CERVANTES: *DON QUIXOTE* [Part II]
    Vol. 29, pp. 203–429

12. KANT: *CRITIQUE OF JUDGEMENT* [Critique of Teleological Judgement]
    Vol. 42, pp. 550–613

13. BOSWELL: *THE LIFE OF SAMUEL JOHNSON*
    Vol. 44, pp. 354–364, 373–384, 391–407, 498–515, 584–587

14. GOETHE: *FAUST* [Part II]
    Vol. 47, pp. 115–294

15. DARWIN: *THE DESCENT OF MAN* [Part I; Part III, Ch. 21]
    Vol. 49, pp. 255–363, 590–597

16. MARX: *CAPITAL* [Part VII–VIII]
    Vol. 50, pp. 279–383

17. JAMES: *PRINCIPLES OF PSYCHOLOGY* [Ch. I, V–VII]
    Vol. 53, pp. 1–7, 84–129

18. FREUD: *A GENERAL INTRODUCTION TO PSYCHO-ANALYSIS*
    Vol. 54, pp. 449–638

Printed in the U. S. A.

••••••••••••••••••••••••••••••••••••••	FAMILY
ANGEL	FATE
ANIMAL	FORM
ARISTOCRACY	GOD
ART	GOOD AND EVIL
ASTRONOMY	GOVERNMENT
BEAUTY	HABIT
BEING	HAPPINESS
CAUSE	HISTORY
CHANCE	HONOR
CHANGE	HYPOTHESIS
CITIZEN	IDEA
CONSTITUTION	IMMORTALITY
COURAGE	INDUCTION
CUSTOM AND	INFINITY
CONVENTION	JUDGMENT
DEFINITION	JUSTICE
DEMOCRACY	KNOWLEDGE
DESIRE	LABOR
DIALECTIC	LANGUAGE
DUTY	LAW
EDUCATION	LIBERTY
ELEMENT	LIFE AND DEATH
EMOTION	LOGIC
ETERNITY	LOVE
EVOLUTION	MAN
EXPERIENCE	MATHEMATICS

MATTER	RELATION
MECHANICS	RELIGION
MEDICINE	REVOLUTION
MEMORY AND	RHETORIC
IMAGINATION	SAME AND OTHER
METAPHYSICS	SCIENCE
MIND	SENSE
MONARCHY	SIGN AND SYMBOL
NATURE	SIN
NECESSITY AND	SLAVERY
CONTINGENCY	SOUL
OLIGARCHY	SPACE
ONE AND MANY	STATE
OPINION	TEMPERANCE
OPPOSITION	THEOLOGY
PHILOSOPHY	TIME
PHYSICS	TRUTH
PLEASURE AND PAIN	TYRANNY
POETRY	UNIVERSAL AND
PRINCIPLE	PARTICULAR
PROGRESS	VIRTUE AND VICE
PROPHECY	WAR AND PEACE
PRUDENCE	WEALTH
PUNISHMENT	WILL
QUALITY	WISDOM
QUANTITY	WORLD
REASONING	

CPSIA information can be obtained
at www.ICGtesting.com
Printed in the USA
LVHW080304030822
725055LV00011B/40

9 781015 248137